Blue Poppies

A Spiritual Travelogue from the Himalaya

Judith Wermuth-Atkinson

BALBOA
PRESS
A DIVISION OF HAY HOUSE

Copyright © 2017 Judith Wermuth-Atkinson.

All rights reserved. No part of this book may be used or reproduced by any means, graphic, electronic, or mechanical, including photocopying, recording, taping or by any information storage retrieval system without the written permission of the author except in the case of brief quotations embodied in critical articles and reviews.

Balboa Press books may be ordered through booksellers or by contacting:

Balboa Press
A Division of Hay House
1663 Liberty Drive
Bloomington, IN 47403
www.balboapress.com
1 (877) 407-4847

Because of the dynamic nature of the Internet, any web addresses or links contained in this book may have changed since publication and may no longer be valid. The views expressed in this work are solely those of the author and do not necessarily reflect the views of the publisher, and the publisher hereby disclaims any responsibility for them.

The author of this book does not dispense medical advice or prescribe the use of any technique as a form of treatment for physical, emotional, or medical problems without the advice of a physician, either directly or indirectly. The intent of the author is only to offer information of a general nature to help you in your quest for emotional and spiritual well-being. In the event you use any of the information in this book for yourself, which is your constitutional right, the author and the publisher assume no responsibility for your actions.

Any people depicted in stock imagery provided by Thinkstock are models, and such images are being used for illustrative purposes only. Certain stock imagery © Thinkstock.

Print information available on the last page.

ISBN: 978-1-5043-7016-5 (sc)
ISBN: 978-1-5043-7018-9 (hc)
ISBN: 978-1-5043-7017-2 (e)

Library of Congress Control Number: 2016919362

Balboa Press rev. date: 12/30/2016

To Siddhartha Krishna

Chapter I

Above the Tree Line

India is like the human mind—it has so many layers! If you learn how to meditate on your own mind, you might discover its ever-deeper and deeper layers, though you will never know how deep a level you have actually reached. So it is with India. It is an ocean of different peoples, customs, religions, philosophies, rituals, smells, and tastes. There is so much of India that a newcomer could easily end up drifting upon its surface—as if sitting on a raft, pushed by the waters of the Ganga, and witnessing only a fast-forward garland of colors, poverty, temples, and affordable luxury hotels.

India to me was not simply a country I wished to see—it was a quest. I became aware of that quest when I was a teenager, but I came to India for the first time when I was fifty. In all the years in between I was preparing—consciously and unconsciously—as though silently guided by a trusted master who had initiated me into a sacred mantra—India. What I desired was not necessarily to see the beauty of the temples, the grandeur of the palaces and mosques. I wanted to learn about the ancient times, the knowledge hidden in the *Vedas*, the thinking of the Yogi, the perception of the human mind and body in the philosophy of the *Yoga Sutras* and the *Upanishads*, and about the sacredness of the Himalaya.

Why all this? I may never know. Some believed it was my interfaith upbringing that inspired my interest in Hinduism—a religion that at its core is most open and most tolerant, though history has demonstrated the opposite as well. To others it was obvious that, having read about yoga philosophy and about Indian mythology, I wanted to see their origins for myself. Many of my closer friends thought I was attracted to the idea of India because of a particular memorable dream I had as a child, and there were even those who told me that by going to India, I might have wanted to return home, to a place from a previous life. I myself have never really cared much about this question. I was living with this quest of mine as a child lives with the love for its mother. But if I had to ask myself seriously why I wanted to see India, I would probably offer an explanation different from that of the people around me.

I believe that I met India high up in the mountains of the country where I was born—Bulgaria. The highest summit on the Balkan Peninsula, Musala, is in the Rila Mountains. It is just under ten thousand feet or three thousand meters. The mountain chains in that country have very different characters. Pirin is full of deep, cold lakes and rivers and has sharp and rocky peaks similar to those in the Alps. The Balkan Mountains are a range that is a continuation of the Alpine chain. It is somewhat lower, but it extends from the border between Bulgaria and Serbia in the west, all the way east, down to the Danubian delta at the Black Sea; the legendary Rhodope mountains, home of Orpheus, form the border between Bulgaria and Greece and enchant the traveler with their mystical river gorges and caves. And then there is Rila, a mountain where one gets above the tree line quickly but that nevertheless is very green, with soft and gentle shapes. Before I was born, there had been a spiritual teacher in Bulgaria, known in the West as Beinsa Douno or the Master. The Master and his disciples spent summertime in the Rila Mountain. In the beginning, each year they used to set their summer camp in a different place, until eventually they settled in an area called *the Seven Lakes*. They used to spend a month or two together. At sunrise, to the sound of songs composed and often played on a violin by Beinsa Douno himself, they performed movement exercises called *paneurhythmy* (in good or perfect rhythm with nature). Every day, after the *paneurhythmy*, the Master gave a discourse on a particular ethical or philosophical topic. The disciples would listen and ask questions. Then they all cooked and ate together, cleaned the trails, rested near the lakes, and prayed. As a symbol of gratitude to the mountain and to nature, the Master and some of his disciples built a small fountain that captured the water running down from a high peak into two beautiful cupped, stone-carved hands. In 1944, as World War II was coming to an end, the communists came to power in Bulgaria. They prohibited the summer camp. Over the next half a century, until the fall of the Berlin Wall, the regime was trying to suffocate Beinsa Douno's movement in an effort to establish an atheistic nation. The members of the community were persecuted, and the reading of books with the lectures of the Master, written down in shorthand and transcribed by the disciples, was strictly forbidden. Beinsa Douno had died a decade before I was born, and I never saw the summer camp of his days. However, I studied his teachings with one of his very first disciples. I read his lectures, and I trekked in the mountains where he camped. It was in the mountains where

I learned most about my master. It was in the mountains where I learned most about myself. It was in the mountains where the concept of the Himalaya was created in my mind and where my wish to go to India and learn about its ancient wisdom was born.

My first trip to India was a trip to the Himalayas. I went to trek there for a month. On the day before the trek began, my second day in India, I went from Delhi to the Taj. I had to take a bus from Connaught Place at five o'clock in the morning. I was staying close to the hotel from which the bus was leaving, and I did not have to take a tuck-tuck or a rickshaw. I walked.

In Delhi, early in the morning, the monkeys used to wake up and start running down the trees in large groups, dozens at a time, trying to escape the inescapable noise of the workday traffic. This was in the days when I first saw Delhi. Since then, things have changed. Legend has it that the monkeys started invading government offices, entering through the open windows, and that they caused terrible damage by playing with or eating the stacks of papers. Since monkeys may not be exterminated in India for religious reasons, an alternative solution was found. Allegedly, the monkeys of Delhi were lured to leave the metropolis and go to more rural areas by another species of Indian monkeys that were not so fond of the big city. Today, there aren't that many monkeys in Delhi.

At the same time of early morning, people who live in the open, outside any homes or buildings, and maybe outside society itself, start moving too. Some of them sleep in parks along rivers—either in groups or as loners. Others spend the nights on top of the small barrows they use to sell fruit and vegetables during the long, hot days. Six, seven, sometimes more naked bodies are pressed next to each other, on a surface no bigger than twenty square feet. It makes one silent.

The bus followed the old Agra road. The express motorway was not yet built. If I hadn't taken that bus so early in the day, I would never have seen those endless human chains, people who seemed to live off nature, together with the street dogs and some bony cows. Other tourists were taking pictures through the windows of the bus, but I could not. It felt as if I would be taking pictures of Christ on the cross.

Some of the people I saw along the Agra Road did seem to get up in the morning and go to work. They washed in the rivers or in the sewer drains beside the roads. Then they took public buses, whose appearance no one seems to be interested in improving. Those who were a little better off might own rickshaws or scooters. They gave others a ride. Often four or five people, including children and pregnant women, would sit on top of each other on a scooter, taking a terrible risk but having no choice.

The Taj, by contrast, looked like a place from a fairy tale. It was as if heaven made it, not human hands. When you approach it, you might think that there could not have been a more beautiful symbol of love. The empress's wish that the world remember the love between her and her husband was fulfilled, but what a change there was—from the landscape of the slums along the Agra Road, which leads to the Taj Mahal, to the image of the Taj itself!

Change in fact seemed to be a basic feature in Indian aesthetics, as well as a basic concept in the life of Indians. I thought of this on the first afternoon after I landed in Delhi. A few hours after I settled in the hotel, I found myself sitting cross-legged in a small carpet shop where I was offered masala tea and called ma'am. A man on the street had invited me to the carpet shop of his "uncle." Going to that shop, on the second floor of a very dodgy building, may not have been very smart of me, but in hindsight the experience was fascinating. The colors and the patterns of the carpets the shopkeeper showed me changed every time I looked at a carpet from a different angle. Later I noticed the same about the colors and patterns of the Taj and the colors and patterns of the saris women were wearing.

Did the same apply to Indian society, culture, or religion, or to their philosophy?

I did my first Himalayan trek with a small group of six plus two Americans and two local guides, a cook, and eight horsemen. This particular trek was organized for the first time a year before I went on it, and it was given up two years after because for many people, it lasted too long. I was one of the few very fortunate trekkers who had the chance to do it.

The trekkers' group met in a hotel at Connaught Place in Delhi. The two American guides were a husband and wife in their late fifties. They had lived in India for over twenty-five years and seemed to be quite familiar with Indian customs and culture. We were supposed to cross the Great Himalayan range from east to west. First we took the train from Delhi to Chandigarh, and then we drove up to the Kullu Valley. In Manali we met the rest of the team, the local guides and the horsemen. On the way up to the higher mountains we visited Nagar, the village where the Russian artist and international peace activist, Nikolai Roerich, had lived, and then we continued to Keylong in Lahaul and Spiti, heading further to the base camp of the Shingho-la pass, and over the pass, to the Zanskar range. After having spent about three weeks in the Indian part of the Tibetan plateau, we got down again to the town of Kargil at the

Pakistani border and ended our trek at Leh in Ladakh.

Most of the time we were trekking at an altitude of fourteen to sixteen thousand feet, with our highest point being the Shingho-la pass at 16,750 feet. We saw very few people during the trek, for most villages we went through consisted of just a few houses. Some of those we met must never have seen people who looked like us. I remember an old woman pulling up the side flap of our dining tent one evening and staring at us in obvious amazement. She did not speak any of the dialects our local guides knew, and they could not figure out why she was staring at us. However, we also met a woman who knew more about people like us than we expected. She invited us to her home. She lived in a village of about twelve huts, very high in the mountains. Her hut consisted of two floors with one room each. Her family inhabited the upper floor, furnished with a stove, two sleeping rugs—one for her husband and herself and one for her child—and some pots and pans. All around the walls there were sacks with rice, which served as a kind of insulation too. On the ground floor lived a cow and two goats. Animals and people kept each other warm this way. The woman spoke to us in English. She had gone to high school in Manali but later had to move to this village because it was the place where her parents found her a husband. When I asked if there was anything she would like me to send her when I got back home, she asked for an Urdu-English dictionary. I had to send it with the guides next summer though, because there was no postal service to that village. The little boy the woman held by the hand while we were in her home was the only child in the village. I did not see him smile. He looked as serious as the harsh winds and the rugged rocks.

We visited Buddhist monasteries where lamas had been working on clay mandalas for years, all done in silent meditation. We saw shamanic Hindu rituals performed by local priests and commoners. Once, we came to a village where a young man had died. The family had asked the priests from two temples to bring two particular gods to their home for the sake of their dead son's soul. Legend had it that these two gods had been at odds with each other for a while. The villagers believed that if the gods were reconciled, young people in the village wouldn't die. We saw the procession of the gods, who rested in disguise on top of shoulder carriages. Each of them was borne by about a dozen men, followed by women with loose long hair, dancing in trance. At a corner the gods met. They stopped. They got upset with each other. The shoulder carriages started shaking. The men could barely keep balance. Two school girls in uniform ran down the street to watch. The saw me, and they saw that I had a camera.

"Can you take a picture, can you take a picture?" they yelled over each other.

"Of the gods?" I asked.

"No, of us," they said, giggling. "You don't want to upset the gods. They can punish you."

I needed time to absorb all this on my own. Reflecting on everything immediately was impossible. During the trek I was not able to discuss what we saw even with the rest of the people in the group. I was focused only on preserving that world—a world that was both fascinating and disturbing. I wanted to store it in my mind and in my heart, as deep as possible. Forever. It was as if humanity had laid out its very essence on a mountain plain and I was there to witness this. But there was also something more to my first experience in the Himalaya, something beyond my perception of humanity.

I have always loved nature. I liked trekking at high altitude, above the tree line, where all you see is mountains, summits, and the sky—perhaps some water and a few birds too. But what I was seeing here, very high up in the Himalaya, in Indian Tibet, when we were a little under seventeen thousand feet, was something very different. The landscape was rugged. There was no more green—no grass, no moss. The endless ups and downs of those mountains looked like a desert of rocks. We could have been on the moon for all I knew. I had no previous conception of mountains like that, or of rocks like that. But I felt some amazing warmth, a powerful embrace. I realized that I was not looking simply at a landscape. I was dealing with a living being—an enormous being—the planet. In theory, I may have always accepted the view that all celestial bodies are beings. But that had been in theory. In the mountains of Tibet I perceived that being with my senses, not only with my mind. However, it was not exactly as if I was one being that perceived another. *I* seemed to be *it,* and *it* seemed to be *me.* There was no real distinction—we were both the same breath, the same love, even the same sensation. I felt something that we might, for lack of a better word, call happiness. And I felt safe—safe because I was part of this being, because there was some communication between the individual me and the *me* that was *one* with this enormous being, our planet.

I was not astonished or surprised. This felt completely natural. It was even strange that I had not lived with this feeling all my life. It seemed so silly that I had thought of *me* as something separate, someone who could like or dislike nature. As if I could like or dislike my heart or my breath! Years later, in a state of meditation, I felt the same oneness with God. But it was the

Himalaya that made me understand *oneness* first, in concrete, tangible terms.

It was the Himalaya that made me understand eventually how to walk on a path of any kind of development—personal, spiritual, intellectual, even professional. There are mountains where you might climb up a steep hill or two, or three, but then you could walk for a while on a plateau, maintaining the height you have reached. The Himalaya is different. You could rarely stay on a plateau for an extended period of time. When you trek there, you have to go uphill and downhill all the time. You reach a certain altitude and you actually have to go down again, only in order to be able to begin your next ascent. To some, I know, this seems not only hard but also annoying. To me, it has been beautiful. Every time I had to go downhill, I knew that soon I would be climbing up again, toward these endless peaks, above the tree line, where the world below would no longer matter, where I was gradually dissolving in the surroundings, in nature, in God—becoming one little part of the universe, of what I did not know. And every time I was climbing uphill, I knew that after the summit, inevitably, I would have to head down again to the places that would bring me closer to human life, to the trees and the meadows, to the birds and the lakes, to the plains and the villages, to what I knew. There has been no major experience in my life that I did not relate to my trekking one way or another. I seemed to apply the transformative knowledge I have gained by trekking to every single process of learning in life. Hope, patience, persistence, steadiness ... I learned all this in the mountains. Most of all, trekking taught me that all one can really do in a critical situation is take one step at a time—carefully. Mountains have been like a spiritual school to me—with their "mountain gods"—the summits that should not be conquered; with the trails one has to break in deep fresh snow; with the fogs in which one turns in circles; with the storms that one may not survive, and with the mysticism of the blue poppies that one dreams of seeing but never touches when they are found, for their beauty is of a world that should be left alone.

Chapter II

"Nice and Clean"

The second time I went to India, I wanted to learn more. I wanted to find a school, a place where I could learn about the Vedas, about the philosophy of the *Sutras*. Reading books alone was no longer enough for me. I wanted a living experience.

I started searching on the Internet. I found many places and many names. Some looked very interesting, and others looked a bit suspicious—as if they were too focused on getting money from Western tourists. I was sad to realize that there were good schools where one could study hatha yoga, Ayurveda, or meditation, but no place where I could go to study philosophy in India, except of course some big universities. I was not going to give up my plan, but I was probably ready to postpone this trip when a strange name popped up in Google.

I had entered the key words Vedanta, yoga

philosophy, and also English. I looked up the name. The site was about a monk, educated in a Hindu monastery in Rishikesh, at the Ganga. He was living in an ashram, he had taught Sanskrit in the same monastery where he was educated, and at the moment he was teaching Vedanta philosophy in the Iyengar Yoga school offered by his ashram. The young man was already known for some of his short articles on yoga philosophy published in an Australian yoga magazine. I thought someone like this monk, who also spoke English, might have more patience and understanding not only for my desire to learn but also for my Western ways. That was important to me because I was approaching things to a high degree on the intellectual level, and I knew I might not be able to adjust to a purely Eastern way of learning or of teaching, though I had no idea what I was really thinking about.

    I sent an e-mail to the monk, asking if I could spend some time sitting in on his philosophy classes once I had arrived in India. The reply I received was very disappointing. All courses were going to end before the time of my arrival at the end of May, since after that, the weather was going to be too hot in India and people would have stopped coming to the schools. Because of the heat, this young monk was going to take his old blind father, who he had been taking care of for many years, to an ashram higher up in the

Himalaya. He was not going to go back to his home in Rishikesh for the three unbearably hot summer months—June, July, and August.

I was very sad. I knew I could not travel earlier in the year because I was teaching and I could never leave before the end of the spring semester. I also thought I was not that young any longer and I did not have too many years to turn this old India dream of mine into reality. What to do? I decided to give it one more shot. I wrote a longer letter to the monk in Rishikesh. I told him more about myself and my personal life. I tried to explain why I wanted so much to study in India and asked if he would allow me to join him and his father in the ashram in the Himalaya for some time.

My family thought this was rude. They could not believe I would ask a complete stranger, a monk in India, whether I could join him and his old, blind father in some ashram, where they themselves were actually going to be only guests, and where they obviously were going to be on some sort of a vacation. I knew all that. Nevertheless, I had this gut feeling that I had to try. The monk from Rishikesh wrote back to me immediately. I was welcome to join him and his father in the summer. I was to go first to Rishikesh, and I was to look at my stay there not as a visit but as if I was "going home." Then I was to travel with him and his father to the ashram in the mountains, where I was going to be the first Western guest and the first "outsider" ever. The people running that ashram invited me because they believed that if I was asking to study, I should be given a chance. The monk was going to talk to me about different topics—every day, whenever he had a few free hours.

I was happy. I do not know how many times I will be saying in this book that I was happy, but at that point I was very happy. There is simply no other word to describe that feeling. After so many years of conscious preparation I was going to live my dream—to study philosophy in India—I was grateful and humbled.

The trip from Delhi to Rishikesh takes approximately five to seven hours by car, depending on traffic. Driving was my only option. After mid-May, when pilgrims start traveling to the holy cities along the Ganga, it is impossible to find train tickets for the two upper classes, and no one would encourage me to travel third class in India. I had hired a driver through a local agency that worked for the American school and the US embassy in Delhi. That driver became a good friend, and we have spent many years driving together from Delhi to Rishikesh, but back then, he surprised me with his thorough knowledge of the history and the politics of the country, and also with his fine sense of choosing the roads we took. He asked me what I might be interested to see and chose the route accordingly. His English was very good, but he did not speak much in the beginning—only if I asked him a question. I did ask him questions, all the time, and I wanted to sit next to him, in the front, unlike other customers who normally sit in the back. I wanted to sit next to him mostly because I get motion sick if I sit in the back. However, I also wanted to be able to look at the road and to talk to my companion. I was so eager to listen to an Indian speak about India. I wanted to know about his family, how he got married, and where he learned English.

Brij-Mohan, my driver, was married and had two children. He was working for the travel agency that made the arrangements for my trip, and he was always ready to drive customers—no matter where and for how long—because he was supporting not only his wife and children, but also his parents and a brother who was out of a job at the moment. Mohan had picked up English just from traveling with English-speaking customers for years. I had taught different languages to different people, and I thought he was really gifted at learning a foreign language.

On our route I made Mohan stop all too often because I wanted to look at different things—a market, a mosque, a cricket field, where little boys and older men were playing together, a vegi stall in the slums, where people slept together with the cows and the dogs—some on top of the stall and others under it. After a couple of hours, Mohan realized that I wanted to see people, streets—just daily life—and he asked me if he should take some back roads to show me small villages. That was exactly what I wanted.

Mohan took me through a Muslim town. We drove slowly, slowly through unpaved streets, past little sheds in front of which men were lying half naked on bamboo beds and children were tiredly crouching on the ground. I asked Mohan to stop the car so I could walk a little, but he thought this was dangerous and continued driving. Gradually Mohan started talking of his own accord. He told me that sometimes, for a month or even longer, he would drive people who did not want to stop at all, except when they reached their luxury hotels. One family of five did not even want to do any sightseeing, he said. They wanted him to drive them from one hotel to another—that was it. I could not understand.

"Cheap luxury, ma'am," said Mohan. "For you, people from the West, India offers cheap luxury."

Around noon we stopped at a "nice, clean" place for lunch and to use the toilet. Mohan knew the "nice, clean" places very well. I went to the toilet first and then came back to the restaurant. Mohan showed me where to order my food and said he would wait for me in the car.

"Aren't you going to have lunch too?" I asked.

"I already did, ma'am, don't worry about me. You take care of yourself."

In the beginning, Mohan never wanted to eat together with me. I was not sure why not. He did work with women in the travel agency, so he could not have considered having lunch or tea with me inappropriate because I was a woman. What was it then? Finally I asked him directly.

"Usually customers prefer to eat separately," he said. "We have different habits. They do not like eating with us. They think we are not clean."

"But I want to eat with you," I insisted. "I am inviting you—come, let's have lunch. Show me what to eat."

Eventually Mohan gave in. He accepted eating with me whenever we stopped on the road—always in places carefully chosen for me, "nice and clean."

A month later, that same summer, when Mohan picked me up from Rishikesh and we drove back to Delhi, we stopped at an old colonial hotel for tea. We approached the door held open by a handsome young man in red livery. I was already walking through the door and feeling the air conditioning blow cool air into my face when I realized that Mohan had remained a few steps behind. I turned back to him and made a gesture that he should come with me.

"He cannot come in, ma'am," said the young man in red livery.

"He is my guest," I said. "I have invited him to tea."

"He cannot come in, ma'am," repeated the man.

"Then I will not come in either" I said, and I started walking out again.

"He cannot come in, ma'am," repeated the man for the third time.

The cool air coming from the spacious foyer with green, plush armchairs and large, open palm leaf fens hanging over them, where we would have had our tea, stroked my neck one more time before I walked back into the blasting heat outside. Mohan was nodding.

"You should have gone in, ma'am," he said.

"What was that about?" I asked.

"That's the other thing, ma'am—Indians do not want us eating with the Westerners either. We are lower class—servants, this means a lower caste. We should not mix with higher castes."

The last city we stopped at before we reached Rishikesh was Hardwar. It was Mohan's idea, but he did not tell me why. We approached the city around six in the evening. He parked the car, got out, and started walking. Mohan told me to stay close to him. There was an enormous amount of people on the streets, all walking in the same direction. I knew that I should be always looking at the ground when I walked, to make sure that where I stepped was clean. Here, however, there was no way to see the ground. If I looked down, I saw only feet in flip flops and the amazing palette of the colorful saris or kurtas women were wearing—as if I was on a huge meadow full of yellow, red, purple, white, blue, and gold—a human meadow. As we walked through the crowd, I thought everyone was in a hurry to get to a particular place, but I couldn't see where people were heading to. Until I saw it. They wanted to reach the river, Mother Ganga. One after the other all these people reached the shore, and then there was no more. They stopped. They stopped walking, rushing, pushing each other. They sat down on the ground, one after the other, and the whole mass of people lowered itself as the sun was going down into the slow golden brown waters of the river. We sat down as well. And then the chanting began—beautiful, melodic chanting with words I did not understand. But I knew that the chanting souls around me were praying—hundreds or thousands—I couldn't tell. Perhaps it was the world. That was the first puja I saw at the Ganga, in the holy city of Hardwar.

Chapter III

Siddhartha

We reached Rishikesh around eight. This is a city situated at the foothills of the Himalaya, on both sides of Mother Ganga, as the locals call the river. Its name refers to one of the aspects of Vishnu, as Lord of the senses. Near Rishikesh, there is the place of the confluence of the Bhagirathi and the Alakananda rivers, the point where the two streams become one, the sacred river Ganga. One of the main routes to the source of Bhagirathi, the Gangotri glacier at Gomukh in the Garhwal region, which is traditionally thought to be the source of the Ganga, begins in this city. Rishikesh is also the gateway for the pilgrimage Char Dham, a pilgrimage to the four holy abodes Badrinath, Kedarnath, Gangotri, and Yamunotri. In the spring, Rishikesh hosts the International Yoga Festival. It is a city of over a hundred thousand people. Come spring, with all the pilgrims and the visitors for the yoga festival, the city is so overpopulated that, on photographs, it looks like a place where the entire world population has gathered, just before the planet explodes.

I have never seen Rishikesh like that. After mid-May, the time when I usually go to India, Rishikesh is quieter and more peaceful—or so they say. Most yoga schools and meditation centers stop giving classes toward mid-May and many of the famous teachers leave the country for some cooler places on other continents or retreat to the Himalayas. However, this is the time when Indian schools have vacation. So, in addition to the pilgrims who keep coming in smaller or larger groups from all around the country, in the months of May and June Rishikesh is full of Indian tourists who could afford to travel, to pay for vacation, and to participate in the most fashionable recreational activity in North India nowadays—river rafting.

When we entered the city, the dim lights had made the colors of the marketplace and the commercial signs above hotels and shops soft and less aggressive. The noise, however, was powerful. There was a lot of traffic, considering the small size of the city. Perhaps 80 percent of this traffic and the noise it produced were due to the scooters—India's most affordable and loudest means of transportation. Mohan thought he knew where the ashram I was looking for was, so we kept driving up the main road. The air was terrible. I wanted to open the window and stick my head out, in order to look at the people and the buildings, but I could not breathe. Luckily, I was too excited about meeting my host and beginning my Indian month to be put off right in the beginning.

As I was thinking what it would be like for me to stay here for a long time, Mohan suddenly stepped on the brake, just in the middle of the road, and pointed at a young man in white, who was standing on the right-hand side of the street.

"It must be him," he said.

It was him. Sri Siddhartha Krishna—my host, who over the next few years became as close as a son to me.

I did not even recognize the face I had seen on the website of the ashram. Siddhartha was standing there in a white robe and flip-flops, his hands put together in front of his chest, as if for a prayer, a beautiful, big smile on his face. I opened the car door slowly and got out into the evening heat.

I wanted to ask the man if he was Siddhartha when he said, "I knew this was you. Namaste!" and he bowed down slightly.

I love hearing the Hindi greeting *namaste*. I knew, since the time of my first trip to India, that this word meant, "I greet God in you." What a profound sense of respect for the fellow human being this greeting expresses! As long as people mean what they say, of course. Greetings, I have always thought, could tell us a lot about the beliefs, the customs, and the mentality in a particular culture. Many of my European friends have asked me if it wasn't terribly superficial for Americans to greet each other with, "How are you?" Cashiers in grocery stores or bus drivers, everybody says that, even though they may not be interested in hearing the answer. It always annoyed me when people asked me that question. I never thought the phrase "how are you" was superficial. There are formulaic greetings established in each language over the course of centuries or even millennia. Some of those formulae disappear with time and are replaced by new ones, and some stay—as if forever. Such formulae reflect deep levels in the tradition of the respective culture—a way of thinking, religious beliefs, or perhaps basic ethical principles. Both Jews and Muslims wish peace when they meet someone and when they part. In Europe people wish each other predominantly a good morning, or a good day or evening. In Bavaria you say Grüss Gott—Hail God or Greet God—and in the Austrian Alps you say "Fuerti," which comes from a phrase that means, "May God lead you". Somewhere in the history of all cultures and religions, perhaps in their very origins, there must have been reasons for establishing such beautiful phrases. Never mind that they may not be always sincerely meant, never mind that they may not be always consciously used. So be it. In the memory of poetry, of songs, or legends, however, they still carry their ancient symbolism, the symbolism of something that used to be reality. In most places of the world such phrases are the rare remnants of oral tradition, and oral tradition is a magnificent expression of collective memory. I do love greeting formulae, and I love thinking about them.

"Namaste," said my host Siddhartha, the monk in white.

He said it consciously and meant each single sound of it. I realized this fact much later, but I felt the immediacy of that conscious greeting when I heard it from Siddhartha the very first time. Can you imagine how you might feel if someone greets God in you? Maybe exactly as one was supposed to feel when that phrase was originally used—as part of God, a loved and respected part of God.

"Namaste," I said and bowed deep down.

In the early 1950s, post-independence India was focusing on a reform movement started by a follower and a spiritual successor of Mahatma Gandhi, Vinoba Bhave, called also Acharya, the Teacher. In his intention to continue Gandhi's fight for *ahimsa* (nonviolence) and for human rights,

Acharya initiated the Bhoodan (or Bhudaan) Movement—an initiative to persuade landowners to give a portion of their land to those who owned nothing. To achieve that, Acharya, like Gandhi before, organized a march throughout the country. The participants were going from village to village, asking individual landowners for their voluntary gift to the poor. The whole idea was not simply charitable. Gandhi had rejected the Western model of social progress that included urbanization and the migration of people toward the megalopolis, which, in his view, meant massive impoverishment. He believed that India could offer a better model to the world, if only some sort of equality could be established in the Indian village, so that it could develop as a flourishing state entity. To achieve this goal, Gandhi thought, the means of production of basic necessaries should be under the control of the masses. In the spirit of Gandhi, Acharya fought for a land reform through voluntary donations of small pieces of land by the wealthy, on which the landless could grow their own food. In the beginning, while India was still under Bapu's spell, many landowners came forward and supported the Bhoodan movement. Eventually, however, the Bhoodan Acts, passed by the governments of some of the provinces, stipulated that the beneficiaries of the small land donations could not use the land for any other but

Blue Poppies

agricultural purposes and that they had no right to sell the plots they were given. This meant that the small landowners were bound to their little plots where they could grow basically only part of the crops for their own use without being ever able to resettle. A strange new type of serfdom was created, and the original participants in the Bhoodan movement were disappointed.

Among the participants of the Bhoodan march, and a close disciple of Acharya, was a young man from a Brahmin family, the son of a Vedic scholar from the Nimbarka tradition of Vaishnavism. When he was eighteen, this young man left his home for the holy city of Badrinath. In Hardwar he met Swami Gangeshvarananda, a master considered in India to be one of the major Vedic scholars. With him he studied the Vedas, living in Hardwar and then in Mumbai. Later, circumstances brought the young man in contact with political figures such as the first Indian prime minister, Pandit Nehru, the president at the time, Dr. S. Radakrishnan, and a French lady known in India as Madame Louise Morin, who was close to the Nobel Prize poet Rabindranath Tagore. Dr. Radakrishnan advised the young man to pursue a doctorate degree at the Hindu University of Banaras. After he completed his education at Banaras, the young man met Acharya and became involved in the Bhoodan movement. Many years later, this man has become known in different parts of the world as Sri Prabhuji. He has traveled and taught both Vedanta and yoga philosophy, as well as Gandhi's ideas of *ahimsa* (nonviolence) on the European continent, in England, Egypt, Turkey, Iran, and Australia. Today, he has followers all over the world. People in India call him a saint because, for almost seven years, from 1973 till 1979, he practiced *vanaprstha*. In other words, he lived the ascetic life of a hermit in a cave in the Himalaya, near Solan—a town close to Shimla, the former summer seat of the British raj. That man, Sri Prabhuji, was the old blind father of my host Siddhartha.

How can a saint, a holy man, become a father?

In his own words: "It had to be, so that this son of mine could be born."

In Hinduism, there are various interpretations of celibacy or *brahmacharya*, a word that originally signified more generally the studentship of Brahman. There are different stages of studentship, as well as different ways of practicing *brahmacharya* prescribed to highly developed practitioners following a spiritual path. For some, a married life includes a particular regime of abstaining from sex for certain periods of time, while others give vows for observing celibacy as long as they live. At some point of his life, after he had spent seven years in the cave near Solan, Sri

Prabhuji met Siddhartha's mother. They fell in love, and they had a son. They were married and they have stayed together ever since, but they did not live as husband and wife—at least not in a Western sense. They both, however, have dedicated their lives to the child they became parents to under such exceptional circumstances, and they both have given that son of theirs all the love parents could possibly give. Siddhartha's entire life is one remarkable example of the manifestation of love—his parents' love, God's love, and most of all the love he gives to others.

His mother, Usha Devi, is today a teacher of Iyengar Yoga known throughout the world. She was from a family of nine children that lived in a small village in the Swiss Alps. Usha came to India in the late '70s. I do not know the details of her interest in this country, but she was obviously traveling because she was, in a way, on something like a spiritual journey, to use this cliché phrase. When I first met her, I was surprised by her tough, resolute appearance and tone of voice. She was then in her early fifties, a short, slightly chubby woman, with beautiful snow white hair, dressed in a kurta in white and red, with a long white shawl—dupatta. Her clothes were freshly ironed and probably custom made. She had amazingly beautiful soft eyes, and she spoke English to me, Hindi to the locals, and Switzerdütsch (Swiss

German) to her son. Usha was limping on her right leg. Knowing that she was an Iyengar Yoga teacher, I was very surprised to see her limp. It turned out that she had been in two terrible car accidents and had twenty-two surgeries, as reported in *The Times of India*. After the second accident, she was thought to be dead by the people who came to "clean up the mess," as they said later. They threw her into a cart with all the other victims of the accident. It was sheer chance that someone noticed she was still alive. She was brought to the hospital, and she recovered. At the time Usha wasn't sure that she would ever walk again. In the mid-1990s she had met B.K.S. Iyengar and had started studying with him. After her first accident, Yogi Iyengar brought her back to life and trained her as a yoga teacher. She started teaching in 2001 and dedicated the rest of her life to this task.

Today, Usha Devi runs the ashram in Rishikesh where her yoga school is organized, the Omkarananda Ganga Sadan. She teaches seven months out of the year, and until her teacher died in 2014, she used to spend every summer in Pune with him—practicing, training, and learning. She has a small staff working in the ashram. Her employees get strict instructions directly from her, and the ashram works like a Swiss clock. In fact, the ashram belongs to "the organization," the International Omkarananda

Institution, which has been involved with a range of activities related to spiritual, cultural, educational, scientific, and social development, since the founding days of independent India. The founder, Swami Omkarananda, has been recognized multiple times for his services to the state, aiming particularly at the improvement of education in the Himalayan Garhwal region. Nowadays, the institution works through a number of trusts and cultural and educational organizations, but its leaders are people who live a spiritual life. They live in a beautiful but modest ashram in Rishikesh, and they lead pretty much a monastic life. Usha is not paid directly for the teaching she does or for running the yoga school and the Ganga Sadan ashram. She has a room in the main ashram on the top of a hill, overlooking the city. She lives alone, separately from her son and her husband. She has all her basic needs covered, but there is no money making involved in her epic kind of work. The money she makes is invested by the institution in different projects in the area. This is today, but it all began when things were so hard for her once upon a time ...

Chapter IV

Niraguna

Throughout my life I have had deep and unshakable faith in God, and, in my small Western way, I have tried to lead a life in his service. God, of course, means so many different things to so many different people.

I grew up as the child of a Christian mother and a Jewish father. My parents each had profound respect for the religion of the other, and neither of them tried to force their beliefs on me. When I was thirteen, I became a follower of the teachings of Beinsa Douno. His school of thought and the movement around him were established in Bulgaria in the early twentieth century and spread around the world, mostly after World War II and the Bulgarian communist coup of 1944. Very early in my spiritual development, I accepted the idea that there is one God and that it makes no difference through which religion one serves him.

The world around me, however, considered

belonging to a particular religion to be essential for one's integration in society. When I was young, I felt like an outsider. In communist Bulgaria, people often called me "the German Jew" because my father was a Jew whose father was from Berlin and whose mother was from Vienna. After I fled Bulgaria illegally, I went first to Israel. There, I was not considered Jewish because my mother was Christian. My eight-year-old son, whom I took with me when I escaped, was called goy in school, the infidel, because he was not circumcised. I talked to friends about the way my son was treated then.

"No problem" said everyone. "You will convert and he will be circumcised, and everything will be just fine."

Fine? I thought. *For whom?* After I had spent many years defending my Jewishness in an atheistic communist country, where practicing any religion was a crime and practicing Judaism equaled Zionism, I found myself wanting to defend my Christian background and beliefs. Most of all, I wanted to be accepted for who I was, regardless of my religious, ethnic, or national background. This, however, seemed to be too much to ask of the free world I had risked my life for.

I left Israel in order to be able to fight for a family reunion with my older son, whom I was forced to leave behind as collateral when I fled

Bulgaria. However, it was impossible to do this while living in Israel since the diplomatic relations between the two countries had been broken right after the Six-Day War. My younger son and I moved to Germany, and soon my older son joined us. Germany was the country of my father, my grandparents, my uncles and aunts. Since I had a German name and since German was one of my two native languages, I was accepted well—as a German. My sons, however, were foreigners—a very specific exclusive category in German society of the 1980s and 1990s. After all the risks I had taken and all the sacrifices I had made in order to take my children out of a country where they were not going to be free politically, intellectually, or spiritually, settling with them in another country where they would remain aliens for the rest of their lives did not feel right to me. So, once again, for the third time, I decided to leave everything behind—my stable financial situation, my excellent living conditions, and my teaching position at the university—and I started all over again—in hope of finding that corner of the world where I could be exactly who I was, and where my children would not have to be ashamed of speaking their native language on the street. This time, I left for America.

I have been living in America for a quarter of a century now. It is true that in the United States everyone is supposed to be at home and that everyone's background—ethnic or religious—is supposed to be respected by law. Yet, in reality, it depends where one lives. If one lives in New York or another big city, that will be mostly true. If one, however, lives in a small town in the South or even in the Midwest, then that may be quite untrue. Particularly the issue of religion is complicated. Today, we talk a lot about religious tolerance, not realizing that simply tolerating each other is not the point. What did I think, then, was the point?

Many years before I went to India, I had given up searching for people who would not simply tolerate me, but who would feel the way I felt about religion. I learned to avoid the question of whether I was Jewish or Christian, and I learned to live without going to temples. Those who realized that I did not believe in the advantages and disadvantages of different religions, or generally in the religious division of humanity, thought I was a confused person lacking any sense of identity. Such interpretations did not bother me. I had my strong belief, and I knew God would not be upset with me because I do not want to use only one of the popular names for the divine. There were a few people who did understand me—my sons, and my second husband. Otherwise, I was a loner. My temples were the mountains and my mind, and this was why I had come to India—to trek, and to cultivate my mind.

I fell so much in love with India that I have been coming back to it for many years now.

This time, when I came as a guest to Siddhartha, I wanted primarily to study with him. Already before I arrived in Rishikesh, it was clear to me that I had found not only the right teacher, but also someone whose understanding of religion was similar to mine. Like me, Siddhartha was also interested in cross-cultural and cross-religious studies. I was already expecting to have an exceptional experience.

My room in Rishikesh was on the second floor of the ashram, which was situated directly at the river bank of the Ganga. In the room there were two beds with fresh, colorful sheets, a wooden table, a chair, and a small wardrobe made of tin. Coming from my apartment in New York I could have been taken aback for a moment by the simplicity of my habitation. But I was not. When a quarter of a century before, my son and I escaped from communist Bulgaria, we had to cross several borders and we had to live in different asylum shelters—first in the UN refugee camp in Belgrade, then in a Beit Olim (a house for newcomers) in Tel Aviv, and later, until I found a job, in an asylum home in Munich too. I had left Bulgaria with one backpack, full of my son's clothes and very little stuff for myself. So, luckily, I was familiar with simple living conditions, with almost no furniture, clothes, food, or all sorts of other things. The time when I was a homeless, jobless, and moneyless refugee had taught me that not all clutter matters. I knew the meaning of the word *survival*, and I remembered that, back then, all that used to make me happy was the fact that after cleaning people's homes, I was able to buy food for my little son. Those times were now long gone. Yet ... had I forgotten them? Had I become spoiled by the good life I had at the moment? Have I ever wanted to forget the months when my son and I could eat just one meal a day?

I opened the door to the terrace overlooking the Ganga. The sun had left. Underneath the terrace there was a beautiful small garden with palm trees and many, many flowers. The Ganga was moving heavily and slowly. Her color was muddy-brown. Nearby, I could see a hanging bridge, full of monkeys crouching on the steel ropes. On the other side of the river there were lights. People were sitting on a platform built in the water next to the bank. They were singing their evening prayers. The sound of the voices was soft but powerful. Did I think then that the Ganga was holy because I had heard that it was or because I was feeling that it was? I did not know. But I knew I had never forgotten the simple rooms of the asylums I went through and my life had not spoiled me. How did I know that?

Blue Poppies

Because I felt grateful for the beautiful room I had in the ashram, grateful for seeing the Ganga and the mountains behind it, grateful for feeling that this was a holy place. *Savlanut* was the word they first taught me in Ivrit when I arrived in Israel. Patience! I had waited for about forty years to find India. Patiently. And finally I was there.

A few days after I arrived in Rishikesh, Siddhartha, his father, and I drove up to a monastery in Solan, the Dada Chellaram ashram in the hills of the Himachal.

We arrived in the early evening. The day was hot and the drive exhausting. A winding, narrow road took us up into the hills. When we were already high enough to have a panorama view of the widespread, densely populated town of Solan, we stopped in front of a small cast-iron gate. I couldn't see yet what exactly was behind the gate. Siddhartha drove in and slightly downhill, until we parked in a small white plaza. My heart was cramped. I had no idea where I was, but I knew that I was certainly not in a hotel where I could change my room, complain about the air conditioning, or leave whenever it pleased me. I knew I was going to be stuck here for a while, and that worried me a little.

I got out of the car. The first thing I saw was a beautiful two-winged white building with a dome. Somehow it reminded me of an open blossom. It was a temple. A gray-haired middle-aged man in white approached and welcomed us. He greeted first Siddhartha's father, touching his feet. I saw the gentle smile on the blind man's face, and I realized that there was trust and love in it. I learned only later that Prabhuji has been coming to the ashram for almost forty years and that he loves it. The man in white came then to me and greeted me in splendid English. His soft but penetrating eyes spoke for goodness and intelligence. *Nice*, I thought to myself. *It might work.* This is how I met Haresh, the son of the founder of the ashram, Niraguna.

We took the steps down to a lower terrace level, where two rooms were prepared for us. I entered my room through a low door with a heavy lock. The room was even smaller than the one in Rishikesh. Similarly, it contained a bare minimum: a bed with a blanket and two pillows, and a table. There was no chair. I got nervous. "Patience," I said to myself, "there is no way out now."

In the next hour or so I tried to organize the luggage I brought—three-quarters of which I never used. The available space was either under the bed or in a niche in the wall. I left the middle of the room empty, put my backpack in the niche and my suitcase under the bed, and thought, *Now what?* There was no power at the moment, and the old plastic fan on the ceiling didn't work. There was a bathroom: a toilet, a sink, buckets to use for taking a bath, and a small water tank to heat up water. *This is good*, I thought. During my first trek in the Himalaya, I had to wash in the rivers, if and when we came across a river. Suddenly, I realized how stupid my thoughts were.

Pull yourself together! I told myself. *You have come here to learn something about spirituality, and all you can think of is what you can complain about! What happened to remembering your past experiences in the asylums? But it is natural, isn't it? Maybe, maybe not! Maybe it is too late for me to learn. Maybe my mind is already so attached to all that high standard rubbish that I won't be able even to relax, let alone to learn? And there is a big spider on the ceiling. What am I going to do with my insect allergies? Why did I really do all this to myself?*

A bell rang to call everybody to dinner, and I had to interrupt this uncontrollable stream of thoughts.

The dining hall was big. Two low and narrow wooden tables were placed in the middle of the room—one for men and one for women. People were sitting crossed-legged on blankets on the floor, something I physically couldn't do. A new wave of panic overwhelmed me.

How am I going to eat?

At that moment a beautiful Indian girl, with

very rich, long brown hair, wearing glasses like me, approached me and introduced herself. She was the granddaughter of Niraguna, Haresh's daughter. She pointed at the tables and the chairs next to the wall, which, in my panic, I had not even noticed. She said that I should let her know if I needed or wanted anything.

"Please, no formalities, okay?" she said. "We just want you to feel well here."

I looked at her deep dark eyes, and I thought, *Yes, I can trust you.*

The first night wasn't easy. I was now hot, now cold, turning the fan on and then off again, opening and closing the door, not knowing whether I should be afraid to leave it open or not. Eventually, sleep defeated my restless mind, but not for long. I had set my alarm clock for four because I knew that the time from four to half past six was time for prayers and I wanted to go to the temple.

I washed quickly, got dressed, and left the room. It was still dark outside. I found my way to the temple and entered it for the first time. It was dark inside too. I wasn't even sure whether I had come at the right time or to the right place, but then I realized that a few people were already there. They were sitting quietly on the soft carpeted floor, cross-legged, and they were praying. There was no "service" yet, there was no program. There was only a silent prayer.

Sikhs and Hindus were praying together. This touched me deeply. It was not a show. No one was going to report about their common cause and their joined service. No media were going to broadcast their concern with God, the world, or humanity. Nobody had organized them. No one was leading their prayers. Over the next two and a half hours, they kept coming—one by one, each for the sole purpose of praying. It was all between them and God alone. A sacred time. I was humbled. And I was glad I could pray with them.

After the prayer time was over, Siddhartha took me from the Sikh wing of the temple to the Hindu wing. Here, on a low white stone pedestal in the center of the room, covered in brilliant starched white handmade lace cloth, there was a book containing Niraguna's teachings—in the form of letters. On the sides of the room, in two different alcoves, there were two other pedestals, which reminded me of altars. On those pedestals, also covered in white lace cloth, there were other scriptures. Their titles were inscribed on the pedestals in large black Latin letters. On the right hand side I read: Mahabharata, Gita, Ramayana; on the left—Bible and Quran. I was in amazement. I was looking at a temple in which the scriptures of some of the best-known religions practiced today were all kept and cherished. Together. I remembered my home city New York on September 11, 2001, and the horrible smell of human flesh burned in the name of what some believed to be a holy war; I remembered the photographs of some of my father's relatives and the stories of their lives—each one ending in a gas chamber during Hitler's genocidal euphoria; I remembered translating the asylum pleas of thousands of people fleeing Bosnia, Serbia, and Kosovo during the last Balkan war—a war stirred partly by another religious hatred between Christians and Muslims. I also remembered wondering, for the most part of my life, whether there was any religious school in the world that does not simply preach religious tolerance but that actually worships all the forms of the one God to whom we all belong and who belongs to all of us.

Sadly, I also remembered that sometimes even sharing the same religion does not really unite us. I was thinking in the first place of Siddhartha. After having completed his studies at the monastery where he spent almost all his conscious life, my friend began to teach Sanskrit there. The death of his master caused the election of a new leader. That person could not wait to send Siddhartha away and to forbid him to teach at his monastery—because he was born to a white European mother, never mind his Indian father. For his white skin Siddhartha was called by some of his fellow monks Chandala—the lowest of the low. Having white skin was even the reason that once Prabhuji, the saint, was not allowed into the Hindu temple Jagannath Puri in the state of Orissa—because he was together with his white-skinned wife and son and was, thus, considered to have been polluted.

I am often reminded of a tale about the life of the legendary Hindu teacher and philosopher Shankaracharya, who is known mostly for propounding the idea that Brahman and the human (or all beings) are of one essence. One day Guru Shankara and his disciples took a bath in the Ganga and started walking to the temple along a narrow road. In the opposite direction, coming toward Shankara, a Chandala (an untouchable) was walking on the road as well. The guru told the Chandala to yield the road to him and his disciples.

"Move away, move away," he said.

"I am my body and I am my inner Self, Atman" said Chandala.

"Whom are you telling to keep away, Achary (Teacher)? This body or the atman which resides in it? Your body and mine are made of the same substance, as pots of varying sizes and colors are made of the same clay. So one such body cannot ask the other to stay away. Are they not part of the same?"

Shankaracharya learned a lesson. Tradition has it that gurus often put their teachings in songs (and something like this still happens today). Shankara started singing a song about the Self that is universal.

"Becoming aware of that is true knowledge, and he who taught me that lesson, regardless of his caste, is my greatest teacher," he sang, bowed down, and touched the feet of the untouchable.

Despite being disappointed by the way the new Swami treated him, Siddhartha insisted that he had profound respect for this man, for the work he was doing in the monastery, and for his scholarship. Nevertheless, my friend was never again able to salute the Swami with *pranama* or to bow down and touch his feet as a sign of deep reverence.

Later that month, in one of the classes taught by Haresh, when, for my sake, he translated the core points of his discourse into English, he said to the gathered brothers and sisters (as people in that ashram called each other), pointing at me, "When she arrived in our ashram, we did not ask her whether she arrived by car, by train, or if she walked. What mattered was that she was here, with us. You should think this way about the different religions too. It does not matter which way we take to reach God—as long as we arrive there."

The gospel says "Love thy neighbor!" As civilization developed we may have learned how to love, but I was wondering if we have learned who the neighbor is. Or do we always pick and choose? And don't we see only those who are similar to us as our neighbors? And isn't the neighbor whom we are supposed to love just about anyone that comes toward us on the road—even Chandala?

The followers of Niraguna, I thought, seemed to have reached beyond the idea of compassion for the neighbor and further to the idea of the brotherhood of human spirituality developed everywhere in the world in the name of God.

All of this I figured out gradually. No one came to preach to me. No one attempted to attract my attention. However, when I did show interest, when I asked questions, they were all there for me—to answer my questions, to help me understand, especially Mala, one of Niraguna's granddaughters.

When she learned that I had spent a few hours reading those of Niraguna's letters that were written in English and were part of the holy text kept in the temple, she came to me and brought me more of his books in English translation. The gentle way in which she supported my interest, without ever trying to impose, was impressive. Conversion was here not the point. Just the opposite. Haresh said once that he was "dead against converting people." At the same time, however, the followers of Niraguna did not keep their teachings secret. They were open and accessible. Anyone could go to the temple and read from their holy book or from the other scriptures. No permission, no initiation, and no baptism were required. They simply offered unconditional access to their wisdom. In my eyes, the people of this religious group did not simply teach and preach respect for other religions—they lived it on a daily basis. This, I thought, was a way for people from different religions and cultures to come together—not by converting and assimilating each other, nor even by tolerating one another, but by learning, knowing, and profoundly respecting the neighbor's ways. Integration in that case—of minorities, of immigrants, of refugees—would mean including the neighbor's ways of life into our own—not imposing our ways on others, nor giving them up.

The ashram in Solan was run by the direct descendants of the teacher Niraguna, or as they lovingly called him, Dada-ji. One of the daughters of Dada-ji was the current head of the ashram, a younger brother was the one giving most of the philosophical lectures on Niraguna's teachings, and the family of another brother was organizing practical things—the food and maintaining the temple and the other buildings. The visitors varied from Sikhs coming to the cool mountains simply on vacation, to dedicated rich donors, to the sick and poor. In summertime there were also some children around. They made the ashram more beautiful and gave it a sense of life, reality, and hope that only children can impress upon a place.

I was welcome to the discourses as well as to the prayers. The languages used for the singing prayers or *kirtan* and for the reading of other texts were either Hindi or Sindhi, the language spoken by Niraguna's family when they left Pakistan as refugees after the partition. At first, I was concerned that it might be very difficult and even boring to spend two and half hours listening to a language I did not understand. But I was wrong. Phonetically both Hindi and Sindhi are quite melodic languages. I caught myself listening carefully to the readings, as if they were some mantras. Maybe this was the effect of the vibrations of words—a notion I learned about much later in relation to mantra theory. Soon, I realized that it did not matter to me whether I did or did not understand the words of the songs. I was simply taken by the beautiful music. The atmosphere created in the temple during *kirtan* could not have left any heart untouched. I learned the melodies quickly and started humming along. Whenever I caught some words, I tried to participate in the singing. But participating or not, I could sit there for hours and listen to these voices—knowing that I was praying too.

The voices of the people leading the *kirtan* did matter though. *Kirtan* is a special kind of mantra chanting or prayer singing, performed by Hindus and Sikhs under the accompaniment of musical instruments—tablas, two-headed mrdanga, pakawaj drum, karatalas or hand cymbals, and a small portable keyboard instrument which Indians call harmonium. It is practiced during Vaishnava devotional rituals in some yoga traditions, during Sikh services, in the Sant tradition, and in some forms of Buddhism, as well as by other religious groups. Everybody who is present at a *kirtan* is invited to participate in the singing, but in a temple there are people who lead it. They usually sit on an elevated podium, in front of the community, surrounded by flowers, stone statues, or other sacred objects.

The few leading voices were so beautiful that I could listen to them in the same way I would listen to Italian opera without knowing Italian. The alto of the head of the ashram sounded as I have always imagined the voices of ancient oracles. Two of the men had lower, bass baritone voices that were very powerful and made me focus on the music completely so that nothing could distract me. And then there was Mala's voice. Whenever Mala started singing and her voice started rising over the temple in the morning, along with the dawn, I could feel, hear, and understand why over so many centuries and in so many religions chanting was thought to be a mystical experience, why singing has been seen as means of going deeper into a devotional practice.

Usually Mala was leading in the musically most complicated songs. Her voice was trained in a particular Northern Indian tradition, as I was told, but this would not have been enough without her profoundly spiritual, inspired, and focused manner of singing. For the kirtan in the morning and for services in the evening Mala used to dress in white—a color that surrounded her beautiful face with a magic kind of light—one could think she was the incarnation of some goddess. Listening to Mala and looking at her when she was singing was like meditation, and the sound of her voice like a prayer.

I realize that no matter how hard I try in this book to describe experiences that are deeply esoteric, and no matter how hard I try to explain the way India has made me learn, develop, and love, I will probably never find the words to express what it means to pray in songs. This has to be experienced in order to be understood. To me it meant to be, if just for a little while, part of that One Universal Reason in whose image human mind was created. In Solan, every time we stopped singing, there was a shift in my mind—a gradual, conscious shift—between that existence within God and the everyday reality, where I was trying to let God exist within me.

In the daily life of the ashram I was welcome to share with everyone else the simply prepared but delicious and healthy food. One day I was standing next to a few women who were rolling the dough on the large counter in the kitchen, and I was looking at them. The woman next to me asked me if my hands were washed, and when I said yes, she took a piece of dough, put it in my hands, and showed me what to do with it. Making bread seemed to open my senses toward some essential components of life, and it had an esoteric effect on me. It reminded me of planting trees, watering a garden, or milking a cow. Sharing with the rest of the women in the ashram the time when chapatti was made was, thus, a big step toward my integration, but also a big step in my own development.

In addition to working together, everyone in the ashram was assigned a particular individual task too. Sometimes one's tasks changed and sometimes they did not. The idea was to do service for the common good, to understand the concept of service, and on a yet deeper level, to overcome oneself. In the beginning I was not given any task. At some point, however, Didi, the woman leading the ashram, must have realized that this could make me feel an outsider. The task I was given was to clean the temple daily.

Can I explain the effect of cleaning a temple?

The idea itself was not new to me. Many years before I went to Solan I was studying comparative philosophy in a philosophical school in Munich called Neue Akropolis (New Acropolis) and mistakenly described as a sect. (I suppose different societies use the word *sect* to define all sorts of groups they do not know the first thing about). The school was founded in 1957 in Buenos Aires by the philosopher, writer, and historian Professor Jorge Angel Livraga Rizzi. Livraga Rizzi's dream was to establish a movement for the comparative study of different philosophical and esoteric schools of thought throughout the centuries, a school that would be independent from any religion or from the politics of any particular regime. Among the many subjects we studied and took exams in, we focused also on psychology, as seen by thinkers in antiquity. In addition to the lectures given by a nice young teacher, we also had times of practice. One of the exercises the teacher gave us was to clean the few rooms of the school. We had to focus and do everything slowly, carefully, and consciously, connecting the cleaning of the place to cleansing our minds. Each time we dusted a table or washed a tile, we also washed away a negative thought, a dark feeling, or a bad wish from our own psyche. At the end, when we finished cleaning, we lit many candles, we sat down, and we celebrated having a clean place and perhaps, a somewhat cleaner mind. We talked, we laughed, and we were in a good mood that lasted for a while.

Now, every afternoon, I was cleaning a temple. It did not matter whether I worshiped the statues of gods and goddesses that inhabited this place. It did not matter that I did not have a profound understanding of the version of Sikhism practiced here or of the strong influence of Sufi philosophy on Niraguna's teachings. It was irrelevant that I was not going to become a Sikh or a Hindu, that this was not the temple of a congregation I belonged to, and that no conversion thoughts had crossed my mind while I was there. What mattered and what made cleaning this temple an unforgettable mystical experience for me was the fact that I was taking care of a place sacred to some people, that I was taking care of a place to which people came to pray, to hope, to believe, to serve the divine. In that place, at least while they were there, these people must be at their best, at the highest state of mind they are capable of. It was a real service and a real honor to take care of such a place. Regardless if it was a Sikh temple, a church, a mosque, or a gompa—I would do it happily.

There were also other forms of service I learned about when I was in Solan.

My cottage was right next to the one where Siddhartha and Prabhuji stayed. The old man was completely helpless on his own. He needed constant care—someone had to take him for a walk, to prepare his food, to wash him, to comb his hair, but also to read to him and to talk with him. Prabhuji talked a little. He spent a lot of time meditating, sleeping, or doing pranayama, breathing exercises. When he did talk, his words manifested wisdom. One could not sit down next to Prabhuji and simply ask about the weather or about his health. He either gave a discourse on a profoundly philosophical question or he conversed in a highly intellectual way. That, of course, required that the person taking care of him should be a highly intellectual person, who would be able to have such conversations. There was only one such person, and only that one person alone was destined to take care of the sage—his son Siddhartha. Siddhartha was both son and disciple. He was the one to discuss the Vedas with, he was the one to take Prabhuji to the forest, he was the one to wash his father, to wrap his loin cloth around his hips, and he was even the one to prepare special satvic food—something the trusted, beautiful Amita used to do when they were at home. Prabhuji did not let anyone but his son touch him, and he did not allow anyone but his son and Amita to cook for him, not even his wife. There was a Nepali man who helped a little, but he could not do more than watch Prabhuji when he was asleep or go to the market to buy fruit and vegetables. Thus, taking care of Prabhuji, especially in the summer when father and son traveled alone, without the housekeeper, meant a twenty-four-hour job for Siddhartha. And that had lasted for many, many years. While we were in Solan, I had to work patiently on something else myself, and since I was next door, Siddhartha would come into my room as soon as his father fell asleep, and we would start discussing the philosophical topic we were working on.

"How do you survive this?" I dared ask him once.

"Well," he said, "when I left the monastery where I grew up, a thought came to my mind that I could run away, leave India, live somewhere very far ... But then again, I would have wanted to do real service, to help the poor, or to take care of the sick ... And I realized that I had a way to serve—right here, at home, by taking care of my own father."

Siddhartha saw my frozen look. I did admire him, but he saw that I was a bit suspicious.

"You know," he smiled and stroked his small goatee—a gesture telling me that he was wondering if I would buy what he would have to say. "You may not believe that, but of all my studies I have learned the most right here—from taking care of my father, day and night, patiently and lovingly. It has taught me more than all the books I read."

Siddhartha made me silent. I had to think. It was true for him—I knew that. But in fact, it was true for me as well. Of all the learning I had done, what taught me most was taking care of my children—patiently and lovingly. Why did it work so well for me, to raise my children, under the extraordinary circumstances we had lived in? It might have all ended up dramatically wrong! I think it was because of my awareness that this too was a process of learning and a form of service. Trying to help a spiritual being start on his path of life? Isn't that real service?

Siddhartha thought the same of our study.

Sometimes we had only fifteen minutes until Prabhuji would awake. And sometimes we could spend a few hours discussing difficult questions. Once, we spent four hours talking, late at night. My eyes were tired and my hand was hurting from taking notes. Despite all that, however, it was so fascinating to listen to Siddhartha, to understand the answers to my questions, or to discover new ones.

"We have to go to sleep, Siddhartha," I admitted, a little bit ashamed that I felt so tired. "I am sorry I kept you so late."

"You did not keep me," Siddhartha said. "What we do here is service, isn't it? I learn too when I teach. And what more could we do than learn!"

I was Siddhartha's first student of Vedanta philosophy. Years later I thought that it was this attitude that allowed Siddhartha to develop into the charismatic but modest teacher that he now is, appreciated by wide audiences for the power of his knowledge and the charisma in his presentations. It is the attitude of a teacher who takes himself for a learner.

A major change in my life in the ashram occurred through the pure heart, the openness, and the genuine love of a child.

Payal, her mother, and her little brother arrived a few days after I had already settled. Payal was the granddaughter of the eldest son of Dada ji and the niece of Didi, the head of the ashram. Payal was sixteen then, tall and very pretty. I first saw her during prayers. She was playing the dholak, a hand drum.

"You play beautifully," I complimented her.

"It is in my blood," she said.

Payal and I spent a lot of time talking to each other. Her honesty when talking about herself, her genuine interest in me, her explicit love for her brother, and her obvious faith in God were impressive. When she learned that German is one of my native languages, she asked if I would be willing to teach her and her brother some German.

The very first morning when the three of us were sitting in front of my "kutia," my bungalow, and I was teaching German to these sweet, intelligent children, I completely forgot that I was only a visitor, that I was a stranger, that I was a Westerner. I was comfortable and happy, and I felt needed there. During the one month I spent in Solan, Payal did much more than this for me. Her sensitive nature allowed her to see through the shell of the self-confident, Western professor from New York, who had come here in order to do some serious studying with her friend, the brilliant Vedic scholar. Behind that shell, Payal saw in me the woman to whom many things in India were unfamiliar and even scary, a mother who was missing her sons, a wife for whom it was difficult to obey the rules and avoid calling her husband overseas, someone who was not quite confident when it came to the life in an ashram, to the ways things worked here—in other words, someone who needed guidance—simple, daily guidance. As an introduction to her role in my life there, Payal took me first on a tour through the ashram. The beautiful bungalows built on different terrace levels unfolded in front of me gradually, step by step, by going up some stairs and then going down some stairs—in the same way as I discovered the teachings of Niraguna—a name that in Hindi means "without qualities."

My wish to come to learn in India seemed to be fulfilled. However, we do not always learn the way we expect to. I came to India to study the

Vedas and yoga philosophy. For the next several years I studied in India far more things than I had bargained for. The time spent in conversation with my friend Siddhartha Krishna went beyond my expectations of obtaining scholarly knowledge from him. They touched the heart of spirituality, the heart of thinking, and basically the heart of the question of humanity. The religious dedication with which this young man takes care of his old blind father, Prabhuji, could make anyone rethink the purpose of human experience. The ethical teachings of Nirguna's followers made me hope that someday, somewhere, in some other era, humanity might actually be united in the love of God. Payal and her brother Tanmay showed me that if children grow up in a real spiritual yet open-minded environment they most likely will preserve the purity of their hearts and thoughts for the rest of their lives, and thus will be part of a better world indeed. Mala's voice, though never recorded, will often sound in my ears when I pray alone—as a reminder that there are others too who feel part of the same one God as I do. The image of my simple bungalow, my *kutia*, will hopefully remind me that I do not need much in order to be happy. That year, I left the ashram having learned a lot, and I knew I was going to carry the sacredness of the morning prayers in my heart forever. Was this a trip to India I took, or did I start a longer journey to myself?

Chapter V

Namaste

It was a warm and humid Indian autumn. The high mountains were already, close and the hills provided some protection from the otherwise unbearable heat. Every now and then, there was even some shadow on the road where they could rest for a while—to stop panting. The man, a small bundle on his shoulders, was wearing only a white loincloth. He was used to walking for a long time for he had done it many times before. But the woman was seven months pregnant and walking under the merciless sun from village to village, day after day, was very difficult for her.

"One more curve and we will be there," the man kept saying, "just behind that hill over there."

Please, Lord, let me survive this, thought the woman, *so that nothing happens to the baby.*

In the early evening, just at dusk, they finally arrived. They had walked about a month. Walking was the way they were moving from one city to another. They had no money and no luggage, except the small bundle with some clothes; they had nothing except each other. The man was older and the woman very young. She admired him; in fact she almost worshiped him. He was responsible. He had fallen in love and had given in to a passion he had not known before. She was now with child, and he was going to take care of her and of the child, for everything came from God. He had left his family years ago, and they were no part of his life any longer. His father would not have approved anyway. His father was a Brahmin, and the son of a Brahmin could not go and have a child with some foreign woman—just like that. She was of no standing, of no particular family—this was not acceptable. To the family the man had lost his mind, and it was not worth worrying about him.

But that same man, the Brahmin's son, had his own standing. People thought he was a saint. Until a couple of years earlier, he had lived in a cave in the forest. For seven years. Near that same village to which he was now bringing his woman. The villagers knew him. They would bring food to him at the cave, and they would sit and listen to his wisdom. There was a small spring near his cave. He liked its water. It was fresh mountain water—clean and delicious. He would frequently walk to that spring and sit by it for hours—meditating, singing, and praying.

People from the village, who came for water too, would meet him there. Sometimes they would wait patiently until he completed his meditation. Then he would start teaching them, in songs, like an ancient guru. They would spend hours listening to him, and when they went back, they would tell their neighbors what guru-ji had taught them, proud of having met him again. The villagers worshiped him. To them he was a learned man, a sage, a yogi, a holy man. And the members of the ashram nearby had known him too. They were his friends. How many nights they had discussed the big questions of the scriptures! Those people in the ashram, they were educated people. They knew about him being close to Acharya and partaking in the Bhoodan march. They knew about him doing a doctorate degree at Varanasi. They were good people. They were fine.

"Are we there yet?" asked the woman, "I can't walk any more today."

"Here, here," he said gently. "We have arrived indeed."

Night had fallen. The thick forest surrounding the few buildings of the ashram made the night look even darker. The evening service was over. He heard the prayer song they sang before a meal and realized that people were gathered in the dining hall for dinner.

"We are home," he said, and saw the woman cry.

Tall and slim, he was the first to appear at the door of the dining hall. He had thrown a piece of white cloth over his shoulders, to cover his upper body. He took off his *paduka*, his wooden slippers, and stepped into the dining hall. His legs were skinny but still strong. Right behind him, covered in a lemon-yellow shoulder scarf, was the woman. She was trying to bend down over her big belly, in order to untie her sandals and take them off. The song had stopped. People were sitting cross-legged on the straw mats at the low tables—members of the family who established the ashram, rich, well-dressed visitors, and some obviously poor people. A man and a woman were just starting to serve the food from big tin buckets—the woman served the rice and the chapatti, and the man the vegetables. One by one, the people who were sitting there and preparing to have food turned toward the door and looked at the latecomers.

"Namaste," said the tall, skinny man at the door and bowed down, his hands gathered in front of his chest, as if for a prayer.

There was an awkward silence in the room.

"Namaste," answered the woman serving the rice and the chapatti a moment later.

She left the tin buckets on the counter, which was still covered with white flour from making the chapatti, and brought the pregnant woman a chair to sit down. "Thank you," said the pregnant woman in English. People began to eat their dinner. The latecomers were served too. The man was eating eagerly and with appetite and did not notice that his woman was barely touching the food. In India, traditionally, one eats with bare hands, using the chapatti to collect the mixed food on the plate and to take it to one's mouth. Indians believe that if we are to appreciate the food, we should use all our senses in order to feel what we eat. Thus, touching the food with fingers was important for esoteric reasons. The pregnant woman had not washed her hands yet. She did not want to eat with bare hands.

The night went well. There was not much talk. The man and the pregnant woman were shown to their room. There were two beds there and a folded blanket on each bed. Sleep was so welcome after the many days of exhaustion that the man and the pregnant woman did not say a word to each other. They were warm, they were fed, there was a place to put their heads down, and they could rest. That was a real blessing to them.

In the morning the man woke up first. In the early hours, just at dawn, he liked to sit in the open, looking at the light climbing slowly up from behind the hills, and he liked to sing. "God and nature, and the world—it was all love, pure love!" he sang.

After they took breakfast in the dining hall, the man was called to see the ashram manager. They had to discuss where to settle for a longer term perhaps. And they had to decide what tasks should be given to them, for everyone in the ashram was doing some service for all.

The office was in a large, spacious room, with a desk and a comfortable chair. The manager was bent down, examining the fruit contained in a big box—one of those customary gifts that visitors would bring, sometimes in addition to a big donation, and sometimes instead of such a donation.

"Namaste," said the man and bowed down, his hands gathered in front of his chest, as if for a prayer.

"Yes, right ..." replied the manager. "Look ... we need to talk ... You realize, you two cannot stay here. This is not a place for things like that, you see. You are not clean any longer, and ... she is not one of us anyway ... This is not acceptable to the people here ... and what about the villagers? Not sure what you were thinking, but this does not work ..."

The slim, tall man stood silent for a moment. Then he gathered his hands in front of his chest, as if for a prayer, bowed down deeply, and said: "Namaste."

Usha and Prabhuji left Solan a couple of days later. They started their next long walk through towns, and villages, heading for a place they did not know; searching for something unexpected; hoping for a surprise by fate and God, and begging strangers in the villages for room and board—every single day. Usha never set foot in that ashram again. But her son, her husband, and I were there when I heard this story.

"How did Prabhuji forgive them? Why did he start coming again?" I asked Siddhartha.

"He is so forgiving," Siddhartha whispered, "and he loves the place. But also, times are different. Yes, times are different now."

"Love never claims; it ever gives. Love ever suffers, never resents, never revenges itself ..." wrote Gandhi in *Young India*.[1]

---

[1] Gandhi, *Young India*, July 9, 1925.

Chapter VI

Puja

Love, of course, is a concept that does not always overlap with marriage. It is certainly not one and the same in contemporary Indian society.

In India, when it comes to marriage, westernization and tradition clash on every single level. Most people in India, as well as many Indian immigrants around the world, are still having arranged marriages. I learned that this fact has to do not only with tradition but also with social standing, prestige, and the old understanding of castes.

My friend Mohan explained to me that he had not even seen his wife before the wedding. To my surprise, he insisted that he really wanted his parents to choose a bride for him.

"Why on earth would you want anyone else to choose your wife?" I asked.

"I trusted my parents," he said. "I never thought that I myself could choose a woman to live with.

My parents knew me better. I was young, I had no experience—how would I choose a partner? Think about it. When you marry in India, you marry not just one person but a whole family—for the rest of your life!"

"Were you afraid to meet your wife—for the first time at the wedding?" I kept asking.

"I was very excited." Mohan laughed. "I was excited to meet her at the wedding, and I have been very happy—all the years we have spent together as a family."

I also heard from two young girls that they wanted their parents to choose their husbands and that they would not even think of any other way to get married. I thought, *Would they be among the happy ones as well? Who can tell!*

Another friend, Jaya, married in her thirties. She was engaged to a young coworker for several years, but they could not marry. Her fiancé's parents could not accept the fact that their son chose his bride himself, without them taking any part in it. Jaya and Singh loved each other. They were confronted with much humiliation on the part of both families, but they were strong and they were patient. At the end, they were fortunate to have the parents agree with the marriage. Jaya had not been so young when she met the man she fell in love with. When they finally got married, she was concerned that having a baby at her age could put her life at risk. She is now pregnant, and we are all waiting for this child to come.

It seems to me that a big part of the thinking about marriage in India, and about many other issues, for that matter, is related to the views of *others*—the extended family, the neighbors, the village, the parents' friends. In other words, there is a terrible pressure based on public opinion because everyone sees himself through the eyes of another. This reminds me of what we call *honor-shame* cultures. In Homeric times, for example, the highest virtue was *kleos*. *Kleos*, best translated as "renown," was something like a status based on the recognition of heroic excellence in battle. A similar concept of social behavior, based on *honor-shame*, is deeply rooted in Hindu culture too.

Very generally I believe that one should not judge about customs and mores in a certain culture when looking only through the lens of another. When we make judgments about customs, we should always consider the logic of that particular culture as well. However, for many years now I have been studying and teaching the connections between ways of thinking in different epochs and different cultures, and I could not avoid asking myself: "What could be the virtue of marriage based on the concept of *honor* or *shame*, that is, on the view of others or on public opinion?"

I have been told in India that due to arranged marriages the country was avoiding the terribly high divorce rates common in the West. I have also been told that in arranged marriages men and women learn how to live well with one another, how to make compromises, how to be more accepting and more tolerant. Indians also believe that there are many love marriages (to use the Indian phrase) that do not work at all and turn into real tragedies. In many of the families I have observed there, I could see what people were trying to tell me. In others I could not.

It was early evening. The sun was setting, and people were gathering for a prayer on the platform placed in the sacred water. Some were stretching their hands out from the platform to put small candles and chrysanthemum flower petals into the slowly moving, shallow waves. Mother Ganga was all in lights and flowers—a millennia-old temple of nature, absorbing rituals, prayers, hopes, sorrows, excrements, and dead bodies.

Above the city, there was the jungle—full of mangos, macaques, snakes, and wild elephants. Amita lived on a hill between the two—the holy Mother Ganga and the jungle. Finally her family had a house of their own.

Amita grew up without a father. Her mother brought them up—five children—by washing other people's clothes. Amita loved her mother, and she cried every time she mentioned her. When Amita was old enough, she married for love. Nandlal, her beloved, was Nepalese by origin. His family had come to India a few generations earlier, and most of the men had served in the Indian army. Nandlal had a shop for children's clothes and later, when a big company bought the land and he had to close the shop, he was travelling around the country, still selling children's clothes. What Amita did was out of the ordinary, but "who would care what the daughter of the washwoman did," as she once said. Three children were born in the young family, and when they were old enough, Amita found herself a job and started working—another thing that was unusual for Indian women of her generation. But Amita was lucky. In a generation when women were not supposed to work outside their homes, she found work in another family. Her job there could not be subjected to the usual descriptions. She became a most important member of that family. She raised their son, and she was like a second mother and a best friend to him. She also took care of the father, who was blind and who was considered to be a saint. Amita was loved, respected, and appreciated, and her status in society changed.

Amita was a woman of faith. She kept all holidays and all rituals in the tradition, but above all she had a sanctuary that was especially close to her heart—Mother Ganga. Amita loved that goddess, and she related to her as to a living being. Every morning around six thirty, before she went to work, Amita came down the hill. She cleaned the little altar at the river bank, lit the candles, and put oil in the oil lamps and on the heads of each of the statues—of Shiva, Ganesha, and Parvati. Every morning she pulled up her skirts a little and walked barefoot into the river. She bent down, took a handful of holy water and washed her face with it.

"Ganga is my love, my mother, and my hope. She has always helped me. Whenever there was something wrong with my life, I prayed to Mother Ganga and it was okay—everything I prayed for was okay," Amita used to say.

Up there in the jungle, this evening Amita's daughter was seeking the refuge of the dark. She was hiding, with a boy she loved. They ran away. They wanted to marry, and they knew that they were safe only in the forest—for if they had gone down the hill, the people of the town would have despised them.

No one was helping Amita. She did not know where her daughter was, nor even if she was alive. Her family knew nothing about her daughter's escape, and Amita did not want the people of the town to learn of her tragedy either.

There were also, of course, the police. Amita

went to them, but they did nothing. Then Amita was advised to bribe them, and they started showing interest. Amita had to negotiate the price. What wouldn't she be willing to give to find her child! And she gave everything her husband and she had saved for the dream to have a home of their own someday. The police took the bribe. Two days Amita prayed at the riverbank of Mother Ganga. After two days the police found Amita's daughter in the jungle. With the boy. Amita had many advisors now, a lot of counsel. The boy had to be arrested on some charges. Amita's daughter was free.

Free for what?

In the days after the young couple was found, Amita could not dip her feet in the holy waters. She hid her face. The social scandal had to be avoided. The daughter's future was at stake.

Amita's daughter was then sent away—to live with her brother who had a job in Hungary. The daughter learned Hungarian. She learned to clean, to cook, to take care of sick people. And then she studied Ayurveda and she learned how to heal people. She also learned how to dress as a European. Mother Ganga had given that young girl her freedom now, but Amita had no daughter for about eight years—until the girl dared to come back home for a short visit. However, she could not return for good. If she did, people might have learned that once she loved a boy of her own choice, and they could have thought ill of her. She could have brought shame upon herself and her family.

Every morning, at around six thirty, Amita came down the hill, from her house between the jungle and the river bank. She cleaned the little altar at the river bank, lit her candles, and put oil in the oil lamps and on the heads of each of the statues—of Shiva, Ganesha, and Parvati. Every morning she pulled her skirts up a little and walked barefoot into the river. She bent down, took a handful of holy water in and washed her face with it. Then she prayed for her daughter, who was far away, to be well and happy.

Chapter VII

Brahmacharya or on Choices

Siddhartha is still unmarried, but he wears white, not orange. This means that he has not given the vow of celibacy yet. He was educated as a monk, and for the fourteen years he spent in the monastery—from age nine, when his father sent him to the monastery, until the age of about twenty-two—he had to observe *brahmacharya*, or lead a virtuous life. He still does. Today, some of the people he deeply respects want him to get married. They believe that if at the age of thirty-four, a decade after he completed his education in the Kailas Brahma-Vidya Peetha monastery, he had not yet made the decision to remain a monk for the rest of his life, then he should establish a family. Being neither fish nor fowl—neither monk nor a married man—they think, is a hindrance on his way of a harmonious spiritual development.

His father Prabhuji, though, the yogi and saint, does not want his son to be married—at least not yet. It was never clear to me whether this opinion was related to Prabhuji's views of his son's spirituality, or to his own need to have Siddhartha take care of him.

Once upon a time there was a young woman who fell in love with Siddhartha very deeply. She met Siddhartha in an ashram whose name I will not use out of deep respect for the privacy of this woman. She and Siddhartha have known each other since they were children. They both spent almost every summer in that ashram. They were good friends. The young woman's father respected Siddhartha as a scholar and had frequently invited him to give discourses on different topics to the community. The young woman herself was extremely intelligent. Because of her genuine dedication to her religion and to the life of the ashram, people thought that someday she herself might become the head of an ashram. In addition, she was not married, a fact that fulfilled the requirement for the ashram leader to be celibate.

The woman realized that she was in love with Siddhartha when he gave his first discourse in the ashram. She was fascinated with his intellect, and she believed that the two of them shared the same spiritual ideas and the same moral values. She envisioned a lifetime of spiritual work together with him. Right after hearing that first lecture, the young woman asked Siddhartha what he thought about marriage—directly, simply, innocently, she actually proposed to him. Over the next few years she had offered him the possibility to work and to publish through the ashram where she played a certain role, and she had promised him that she would never stand in the way of his spiritual work, whatever that might involve. Siddhartha was not ready for marriage. He was not even sure if he would ever marry or if he would take the vows of *brahmacharya* or continence that often includes celibacy. He was just starting to work as a teacher of Vedanta philosophy, and he was also the only one to take care of his blind old father. Siddhartha could not even begin to think about starting a family. Both the young woman and Siddhartha talked to me about all this.

"I may decide to stay a monk forever," said Siddhartha.

"I will wait for him, even if it takes many, many years," said the young woman. "If it isn't him, there will be no one else. He is my only love. I can never love another man. "

The woman waited for years. At the end, after Siddhartha made it clear that he would never marry her, she did not want to talk to him anymore. She did not want to talk to me either—for I knew too much.

"Do you know what you want to do about all

this?" I asked Siddhartha recently, playing my role of his "Western mother."

"India is my home and my future," Siddhartha said. "But when Prabhuji is no more, I want to go live in my mother's country for a while, in Switzerland, where I could be free from any social pressure, and I would not have to decide whether I should be married or I should keep celibacy for the rest of my life. I am not ready for such a decision and I do not wish to make it, but Indian society is not ready to give me the freedom I need—the freedom to make my personal choices—whenever I am certain of what I really want."

Choices are not simply an expression of our freedom of will. Making choices is the way we form ourselves, the way we develop. By making choices, we create our views, dreams, and visions. We reinvent ourselves with each single choice we make.

In the sixty years I have lived, I have had to reinvent myself through making choices so many times that, today, it is hard to remember how all this came about.

I discovered the power of making choices when I was quite little. I grew up in a very interesting family, in which, however, there was almost never peace and quiet. My mother was a very talented artist and a highly educated person. It was exceptionally interesting to listen to her explanations about art, history, theater, or literature. However, she always managed to stage some arguments and dramas, and there were also real family tragedies. My father was trying to cope with all this. He had married quite late, ten years after the war was over, and he had gotten out of the Bulgarian labor camp where he was sent as a Jew.[2] I was his only child, and I was born when he was forty-six. So, he did not divorce my mother, mainly because he did not want to lose me, but also because he had a very strong sense of responsibility for and of loyalty toward his wife. In any event, often when I was little, I would wake up in the morning, thinking that I did not want to remember the drama scene, the pain, and the offences of the night before. If I had to stay there, in that past day, I might not have wanted to live at all. But it was difficult to always find something in the current day that would make me smile. I did not know what was going to happen once I opened the door of my bedroom—if my mother would be still angry with my father, if she would still not talk to me, or if she would forbid me to play with my friends outside. What I knew was that I needed to find something to smile about, something that would

---

[2] During World War II, the Bulgarian King Boris III, officially an ally of Hitler's Germany, managed to avoid the deportation of Jews to the death camps but had to establish labor camps within the country.

make me happy and allow me to dream about another life, a beautiful, peaceful, happy life. And somehow I figured out that I had to change the order in my mind. I could smile and I could be happy if I thought about that other life. As soon as I focused on it, I was out of the day before, and I was in the future, but that future was actually the present of my mind. Thinking was my savior. The more concrete outlines I imagined for that beautiful future life of mine, the more I liked myself in the present. Why did I like myself? Because I was hopeful and I liked my dreams. Because this was how I chose to think of me—I chose the happy Me.

It was my violin that made things much easier. I started using the "choosing-how-to-think" method of getting out of the horrible days of my early life quite consciously. But one also needs to be able to get rid of certain memories, for they are also very powerful. I had to be able to forget the words that hurt, the disturbing images, the tears … I realized that if I started practicing a piece of music I liked and if I focused on a particular passage that I had not yet mastered, then the wordless concentration on my music would eradicate my thoughts, my memories, the sad images, and it would transport me into a state of experiencing something else—in this case the beauty of the music I was playing. In this state, I was able to perfect something that was difficult, a trill, a chord, some arpeggios—and the perfection was only up to me. After a few hours of clearing my mind in this way, of replacing the ugly daily life of yesterday with the perfection I had achieved in a small piece of music, with my own hands, I could move on to working on perfecting my dreams of the future and, with it, of perfecting my current mode of being.

Was I then the kid of yesterday, who cried, who hated everyone around? I was not. I was someone who was going to be loved and to love—someday—and I was someone who believed in this at the present moment. That, I think, was my choice.

A long time had passed between those early stages of discovering some forms of meditation and my first arrival at the Swami Rama Sadhaka Grama, the Swami Rama village of spiritual seekers.

I had heard from Siddhartha about this ashram, or the meditation center, as it was called as well. After he had lost his teaching job at the Kailas monastery, because he was not of pure Indian descent, the head of the Sadhaka Grama, Swami Veda Bharati, the successor of Swami Rama, invited Siddhartha to teach Vedanta philosophy in the center. Siddhartha spoke very highly of Swami Veda and generally of this ashram, and he felt honored to be teaching there.

My first visit to the Sadhaka Grama was very brief. Siddhartha brought me there for just about an hour. I was immediately taken by the outward layout of the place. Instead of bigger buildings that could host more visitors, here I found small individual cottages spread around an exceptionally beautiful garden. India's climate does not allow for much gardening, except higher up in the mountains perhaps. Beauty has been created mostly in the form of clothes, carpets, jewelry, and certainly in the magnificent temples and statues of gods. In the Himalayan yoga tradition of Swami Rama's village, though, no individual Hindu gods were worshiped. There were statues of Lord Shiva, of the white Tara (a Buddhist goddess), of Mother Mary, of the Buddha, and of other important figures from all religions. However, generally, yoga philosophy is not a religion. Thus, this ashram has no particular temple. It is one of the main world centers of dhyana-yoga instruction, as well as an international center for the scientific research of yogic meditation. The beauty of the ashram here was different. It was created of nature itself. The well-designed rose beds alternated with magnolia, rhododendron, and poppy, but most of the alleys between the cottages were flanked with nicely hedged green shrubs. Just quarter of an hour away from the busy and quite polluted city of Rishikesh, in the midst of a dry and sandy landscape, along a back road where the scooters, the tuk-tuks, and the rickshaws steadily raise clouds of dust, the garden of Swami Rama's village of seekers stretches its long, flower-decorated body over a few square miles, soft and gentle, ready to embrace the guest of this oasis with its calm, and to inspire contemplation. I was sorry I had to leave. I wished I had arranged to stay there for a while.

Usually, I go to India in May and June. May is already a very hot month there. The monsoon comes to the northern part of the country in the first part of June. This means that I have been in India always out of the tourist season, a fact that has both advantages and disadvantages. On one hand I have avoided the crowds and the high prices. On the other hand, I also have missed the kind of people I would have been interested to meet. Many of the good teachers, who speak English too, teach outside India in the summer. To avoid the terrible heat, they usually leave the country toward the end of April or the beginning of May. I was lucky that, because of his father, Siddhartha rarely traveled and that I could spend so much time with him and with the people around him, whom today I call my Indian family. In addition, in the months when I visit India, Siddhartha is more available to work with me, since he does not teach any other classes. In this part of the year, I also meet more Indian travelers who are either on vacation or on a pilgrimage to the sources of the Ganga. All that has made me feel that I was not just a tourist but that I was living a more real life in India. However, when I arrive in Rishikesh, all yoga philosophy classes are already closed, and all teachers who teach them are gone.

The summer of 2013, however, was an exception.

I arrived in Rishikesh a bit earlier, in the very beginning of May. This was because I wanted to trek in Sikkim, and I knew that after mid-May the weather there was not going to be good. The idea that the weather in Sikkim changes around mid-May turned out to be wrong. Local people told me that the climate in this area has changed dramatically, and that now it was already almost impossible to trek in Sikkim by mid-April. So instead of going to Sikkim, I did the Sandakphu trek through Nepal and India. The weather was terrible. I managed to get a glimpse of Kanchenjunga, but after my guide lost me during a hail storm, I cut my trek short and went down to Darjeeling a few days earlier than planned.

After the trek I flew to Delhi and drove straight to Rishikesh. Siddhartha told me that Swami Veda of the Sadhaka Grama had not yet left for the summer, and that he would like to introduce me to him. My interest in Swami Veda was twofold. In the first place I knew that he was very important in Siddhartha's life. There was even some talk about Siddhartha being considered as a possible successor who could lead the ashram in the future—something that was not set in stone but that spoke volumes about the relationship between the two men. Siddhartha shared his thoughts and questions with me, and he even sought advice. To be able to even talk about such a plan, I had to meet the swami.

At the same time, I had also a very personal interest. I had been practicing meditation for many years, but I had never had any other guidance than that I found in books. Basically, with the exception of the few summers when I had the opportunity to work with Siddhartha, my entire knowledge of yoga philosophy, as well as of meditation, was based on books alone. All this never bothered me. My knowledge of the teachings of Beinsa Douno, which were essential to my life, was mostly based on books too. When I met Swami Veda that summer, for the first time a wish was born in me—a wish to have guidance from a living teacher, to ask questions, to listen to someone who "knew" what I was only struggling with.

Swami Veda was sitting on a divan, leaning against a few big pillows. The light in the room was soft and dim. He was wearing his orange swami-gown and at first, looking at him from a distance, it was as if I was looking at the sunset outside—a round, cross-legged orange spot, sinking in the gentle light, as if gradually leaving the room or the day. When Siddhartha and I approached him, however, the whole picture changed. It was interesting to realize that I stopped being aware of visual impressions. I had only a feeling—a feeling of being embraced by some calming power. This was not some psychological reaction. The power was physical. It touched my body, and every single muscle in me relaxed. My face relaxed, and I smiled. (Have you ever realized that when the muscles of your face are completely relaxed, you actually smile—even if very slightly?) For a moment my mind was empty, as it is during meditation. Then I saw it—I saw Swami ji's smile.

I like looking at people's eyes, hands, and smiles, and I had seen so many different smiles. Visually, Swami Veda's smile was like the smile of a child. It made me think of how my children smiled. My older son has this sweet crooked smile. He is a very strong, rather tough guy, but sometimes, when he is embarrassed, or when he wants something and doesn't dare ask for it directly, then at one corner of his mouth, either the left or the right, both the upper and the lower lip go up. The other side of his mouth does not move at all, as if one part of him pretends that nothing has happened and the other part admits that something did happen. My younger son smiles on both sides. When he does, his face looks symmetrical, and his mouth has the shape of a new moon. The most typical kind of a smile for him is the one he has when he has done something wrong or when he has forgotten what he promised to do. He tilts his head sidewise, to one of his shoulders, his eyes, which otherwise always look straight at you when you talk to him, look down to the floor, he smiles just a little, and his voice becomes quieter than ever. It is as if he tells you, "I know you are not going to be upset with me and you will forgive me, just because I am so sweet and because you love me so much."

However, Swami Veda's smile was different from any other smile I had seen before. It was a smile in process. In other words, it kept changing, and it was expressing various things. Everyone's smile may express different things at different times, but Swami ji's smile was speaking to me every single instant. Perhaps his smile was so expressive because he did not speak in words. A couple of months before I met him, he had taken a vow of silence. He was going to keep silence for five years. Silence is a very big topic. Here I shall say only that when I was looking at Swamiji's smile that day, I realized how little attention we pay to means of expression other than speech. Deaf people must see and understand gestures and facial expressions much better than those of us who speak. Obviously I do not mean to say that we shouldn't be speaking. What I mean to say is that once in a while, we should change the set of senses we use to perceive the world—that is, if we would like to operate with a wider scope of sense perception abilities, and if we wish to have a less restricted view of the world and of each other.

When necessary, Swami ji communicated with the help of a computer. He was typing on a small laptop, which was attached to a bigger screen where we could read what he had written. We talked about my work, about Minneapolis, the city where he and I had both lived years before, about my interests, about the Vedas. During the entire conversation with Swami Veda, his smile remained to me the most powerful and most important part of our communication. From a nice, welcoming gesture that made me feel comfortable and able to open up, the smile turned into some kind of a spiritual power. In a strange way, that power, which originated in one individual, was transferred to the other two people present in the room, to Siddhartha and to me. There was some transition from the one individual to the whole aura of the place. It was as if this wave united us, and the three of us became one little field of smiling energy. But what was the energy that Swami ji's smile created? It made me so happy, so inspired, so trusting, so strong—as if I had taken some sort of a life-bath. My mind was cleansed, my heart was cleansed, perhaps not forever but at least for the time being. I turned to Siddhartha and wanted to tell him how I felt.

"I know, I know," he said. "It is overwhelmingly beautiful to be in his presence, isn't it?"

I spent a few more days with Siddhartha and my Indian family in Rishikesh. In addition to Siddhartha and his father, this family consisted of Amita, the woman who raised Siddhartha and became his second mother, her Nepalese husband Nandlal, and one of their three children—their daughter Esha. The other two children, their son and their younger daughter, lived abroad. Siddhartha, Amita, Nandlal, and Esha opened up to me in a way that made it possible for me to live in India as if I were at home.

To return the kindness, in 2013 my husband and I invited Esha to visit us in London where we spend the summer. We sent a formal invitation. Esha had never dealt with any kind of formalities, except perhaps at university. Before I went to India that year, we talked on the phone almost every day, to clarify what needed to be done and how everything was going to be arranged. Siddhartha helped with filling out the visa application. Eventually, Esha took a trip to Delhi to submit her documents to the British Consulate. I arrived in Rishikesh two months later. Esha was still waiting for an answer. Every single day we discussed some of the details of the application process, whether the forms were filled out correctly, and how long we might have to wait.

"Once we are in the UK, you probably could go visit your brother and your sister in Hungary for a couple of days," I suggested, forgetting that the UK did not sign the Shengen Agreement.

Esha and Amita were very patient, but the rest of us were so nervous, having waited long enough, that we had to do something to make us feel better. We started preparing Esha for her visit in London. I described the English climate in the summer and advised her on the kind of clothes she should pack.

"Can I wear a kurta in London?" Esha asked.

"London is full of Indians and Pakistanis, and they all wear their national clothing—whatever it may be. No one would think you are strange," I said, thinking hard if I was really right about that. It amazed me how many things we actually do not know exactly about the places where we live.

"How beautiful!" Esha said. "I will be in the West, but it will be as if I were at home."

Most of the time we spent working on Esha's English, but the girl was so overwhelmed with dreams about the upcoming trip that she could hardly focus on grammar.

Several years earlier, Esha's extended family and particularly one of her uncles, who was a successful businessman, wanted her to get married. However, Amita, Esha's mother, had different ideas. She was not certain what was right and what was wrong for her daughter. She knew that Esha wanted to be educated, and she was not sure if she had enough knowledge to give her child advice about such a big decision. Most of all, she was not sure how to oppose the pressure coming from her brother. Being remarkably intelligent, Amita was analyzing her own life experience, looking for some answers about her daughter's future. Amita herself had found a job when she was very young, and she knew the value of work and of being able to support oneself. She wanted her children to have that opportunity too—to work and to support themselves—but she wanted them to have a life better than her own. She thought that it was important to have education and a profession, and she was inclined toward a more modern attitude regarding women who work. But in some respects Amita was also a very traditional woman and did not want her daughter to follow the cheaply purchased Western models of living and of behavior, which were popular among the younger Indian generation. So, she decided to seek advice. One day, when I was in Rishikesh, Amita asked me if Esha could discuss with me some important issues related to education. Looking in the eyes of this beautiful, still relatively young woman, I saw a deep motherly concern, a cry for help, and I saw the hope that she could have a dream—at least a dream for her child's future.

I met Esha in the pretty little garden of the ashram where Siddhartha always has me stay. The weather was already hot at this time of the year, but there were a few morning hours, when the palm trees in the garden and the light breeze coming from the Ganga, which was just a few steps away, made it very pleasant to sit on the bench, at the little table.

Esha and I had a long conversation. Her choices were quite clear: getting married, something her uncle wanted her to do; going to university and studying computer programming, something most of her age-mates advised her to do; or studying language and literature and becoming a teacher. When she mentioned the last option, she was not looking at me. Her eyes were fixed at some distant point, outside the ashram, outside the garden, beyond the river Ganga—somewhere far away, perhaps at a vision she had of herself.

"Since I was a child," she said, "I have always wanted to be a teacher. I wanted to hear people calling me *Teacher*, not Esha. I want to teach children, young women. Teaching has been my dream," she kept repeating, as if the words *teaching* and *teacher* were a sacred mantra echoing through her life.

Esha found in me the right person to support her teacher's dream. I had been very happy teaching all my life, and it was not difficult for me to convince her that she should follow her dream if she wanted to be happy. Esha decided to trust me, and from that moment she started calling me *Mum*.

Esha completed a master's degree in Hindi language and literature. She chose Hindi rather than English, because she wanted to teach her own countrymen and -women their own beautiful language, so that they could speak and write in it well.

"If they can do this," Esha used to say, "they will have choices."

Inviting Esha to spend two months with my husband and me in London was my present for her graduation. I wanted her to learn about my world, to see something different—beyond what she already knew. When I told her this over the phone, she was ecstatic.

Waiting for Esha's visa in the summer of 2013 became unbearable. No one could be sure how long it was going to take until we received any answer. Therefore, after Siddhartha finished teaching his courses for the season, we all decided to leave together for an ashram in Takoli, high up in the mountains, in the Kullu Valley. We were determined to make this journey a fun journey, to have a good time, and to uplift Esha's spirit because she started getting more and more nervous and sometimes even desperate.

The trip took us about fourteen hours. We traveled with two cars—Siddhartha and his father were ahead. I decided to drive with Amita, Esha, and Nandlal. We made several stops to have chai with the eggless pancakes that Amita had prepared for the road. We talked a lot, we laughed a lot. We made plans about Esha's stay in England—how exactly we were going to make chapatti on my gas cooker. Esha enjoyed the trip, even though most of the time she was motion sick.

Once you get close to Manali, you know that you are in the mountains. The road to the ashram in Takoli was winding, old, and quite narrow at times. Toward the end of the trip, it was not quite clear to us whether there was any road to follow at all. Even Siddhartha, who had been there before, got confused. We had to call the manager to meet us and lead us up to the ashram.

This was a very particular ashram, certainly not one of those that serve as lodges. I was invited there only because I was a guest of Siddhartha's. Regardless, there had been a long discussion about my visit. Basically, the ashram was meant to be a place for serious spiritual seekers who came not on vacation but to practice meditation, to keep silence, and to pray. There were not many guest rooms there because there were not many guests. Only Siddhartha's vouching for me had made the reluctant manager accept me in the absence of the swamini—the woman who built the ashram, and who was in Europe at the moment. The presence of Esha's family was an exception too. They were all taking care of Siddhartha's father Prabhuji, and that was the only reason for accepting them.

When we approached the ashram, I could see only the farm field and the garden. We parked the cars at the bottom of a hill. Behind us, there were two beautiful young cows—the cows that gave us our milk over the next several weeks. One of them was light brown with white spots, the other black. I had not seen many farm cows in India. The holy cows one sees on the city streets look meager and stupefied. They are not fed. They are all skin and bones, and they are just strolling slowly or lying around in resignation in the drought heat of the cities, not even trying to steal food from the passers-by, as monkeys do. The two cows in Takoli were different. They had their own pasture in the field around the ashram, they were well fed, and they were given water regularly. They looked happy, as I could see in their relaxed and curious eyes. The field, as it turned out, was an organic farm with many fruit trees and vegetables. Around the main building, there was a gorgeous, lush garden with roses, poppies, rhododendron, and all sorts of other flowers. In two or three different places behind the field there were small construction sites. One could not see the main building right away.

First I saw only the foundations—solid stone foundations—and a very complex system of water-filtering terraces in the front. Then the main entrance was revealed in the midst of colorful flower shrubs, at the end of a white sandstone platform. Once I climbed the steep steps to the last terrace, the real scale of the building was revealed in front of my eyes, as if I had to climb a holy mountain in order to see the sunset from its top. This was not a small building. The main impression was of the color white, but there was also dark brown carved wood used in the building, as in a Swiss chalet. Simple, but so extremely beautiful that I exclaimed spontaneously, "This is paradise!"

My cliché phrase turned out to be expressing a sense of the place that was truer than I could have thought.

We settled in our simple but beautiful rooms. The ashram was kept extraordinarily clean.

"This is how Swamini ji wants it," said Vineet, the smart, dark-haired young man who was running the place as a manager.

We had the ashram to ourselves, but Vineet always kept an eye on us, to make sure that we were alright and that things were done the way Swamini ji wanted.

In Takoli I felt as if someone had picked me up from an area thick with smog and had placed me in the vacuum of some world of clean air and thoughts, of fresh smells and tastes, and of the feeling of happiness that I was alive.

I suggested that we take turns cooking.

"But the fun is to do everything together," Siddhartha said, and he was supported by everyone else. We did almost everything together during the day. We peeled the vegetables, cleaned the rice, mixed the dough for the chapatti, which Esha knew best how to roast, walked to the market, carried the buckets with milk, picked herbs in the garden, and traveled in the vicinity to visit ancient temples. In the quiet afternoon hours, Siddhartha and I were studying in the library—a spacious white room with huge windows looking at the five peaks surrounding the ashram—five Himalayan gods.

As an exceptional privilege, Vineet would sometimes open Swamini ji's quarters, which otherwise were locked, and he would let me do my practice in her meditation room. At four we always had chai. Amita taught me how to make it, and the two of us took turns.

"A biscuit?" she would always ask.

"I would never say no to a biscuit," I would always answer.

In the evening, before dinner, we would go upstairs to the temple, take off our slippers, and do puja. Every day, Vineet changed the dress of the mother goddess—the beautiful small statue he and Swamini ji had designed and ordered from a sculptor in the South. Siddhartha played the harmonium and sang traditional kirtan. His soft baritone voice was quiet but had volume. We all sang along—in a quiet, shy accompaniment. Often, we sang for so long that we forgot it was time for Prabhuji to have his dinner. At the end of the puja, after all of us left, Vineet would usually remain in the temple alone—perhaps to pray for his swamini who, at the time, was ill, or for his wife who was angry, or for the God Mother who loved him. Once in a while, when Prabhuji wanted to spend the night outside, we would gather around the *havan kunda*, the fire altar in the garden, where Prabhuji would sit on a blanket and sing wisdom to us, like an old Rishi, often for hours.

Little by little I learned the story of the ashram. I learned that the swamini who built the ashram, Swamini Vidyaprakashananda, had once received a task from her master, Swami Omkarananda, to build an ashram in the Himalayas, that would be like a paradise for those who come to it.

Swami Vidyaprakashananda had been a disciple of the teacher, philosopher, author, and mystic Paramahamsa Sri Omkarananda Saraswati ever since he settled in Switzerland in 1965, following persistent requests of Swiss academics. Being an academic specialized in comparative religion herself, Swami Vidyaprakashananda was deeply impressed by the remarkable intellect and knowledge of Omkarananda, as well as by his charisma as a spiritual teacher. She became his right hand in dealing with the ashram's administrative and legal issues, and in the persistent ideological fights with the conservative and hostile Swiss government that feared the growth of what they saw as some unknown, questionable sect in the town of Winterthur. The life of her master, however, was dedicated not only to the writing and the lectures he gave on numberless spiritual topics but most of all to the establishing of different institutions that, in his view, would promote the spiritual advancement of humanity. In addition to building ashrams and temples in Germany, Switzerland, England, and of course, India, Omkarananda had a particular interest in education and the improving of the backward learning conditions of children in the Himalayan Garhwal region. As a consequence of his active involvement with education, today the Omkarananda Institution in India is the patron of over fifty schools, an Institute of management and technology, a few colleges, and two schools for traditional Indian dance and music in this area.

Trying to follow the teachings and the spirit in the life of her master, Swami Vidyaprakashananda, who had lived in India for over twenty-five years, decided to invest all the strength she had left, and all the money she had ever saved, into building an ashram that would serve both the needs of people profoundly devoted to spiritual development, as well as the needs for education of children, women, and the poor in the region where she chose to build—the Kullu valley.

She moved to the Kullu in 2008. She bought a large piece of land high up in the mountains, surrounded by five high peaks, or five gods, as the local people see the summits. Since as a foreigner she could not own land in India, she established a charitable trust in the name of her master and called the new ashram project Omkarananda Maha-Tripurasundari. Swami Vidyaprakashananda was in her late sixties then. She did not speak Hindi, and she had no car. The most important help she needed was someone who spoke good English and could interpret for her, so that she could communicate with the local people, hire builders, place orders, and start moving on with her gigantic project. This is how she met Vineet—the young, intelligent, dark-haired man who was now the manager of her ashram. Vineet was the son of an educated local man who was translating books on Hindu philosophy and had his own teachings and his own disciples. Vineet's English was excellent. Swamini ji liked his mind, his dynamic nature, and his inclination to spirituality. Soon after she hired him as an interpreter, she asked him to be the manager of the new ashram. For several years the young man and the older lady worked together day and night. Vineet was not simply efficient. He understood the European woman's ideas of architecture and admired her knowledge of architecture and of engineering. Together they built the main building, the complicated water-filtering terraces, and the meditation hall and started working on the organic field. They also designed and built the temple together and ordered the statue of the God Mother from a sculptor in the south. These were epic times. They had to hire and to fire builders, they had to choose the few people who would maintain the main building, and they had to establish some relationship with the suspicious local people, who were not ready to welcome a foreign swami into their quite traditional shamanic world. Vineet and Swamini ji had also to survive the harsh winters in the mountains. Sometimes they argued. Sometimes Vineet did not feel appreciated enough. And sometimes Swamini ji did not feel understood. Nevertheless, the ashram grew in front of their eyes, big and beautiful, and they knew they had done a service in the name of God, and in honor of a great master.

But Vineet was young, and his mother was worried about and jealous of her son's devotion to a white older lady who might have had too much influence on him. Thus, she found her son a bride. One day, under his parents' pressure, Vineet agreed to marry, not realizing that the wedding and the bride had already been prepared. Two weeks later he was already a husband. His home was not too far from the ashram, and for a while, he continued his work in the ashram. However, when I met Vineet, I realized that there were times when he came to us from home in a terrible mood—sad and upset. He was a shy young man, but I had worked with young people for years, and I was glad to be able to make him open up. His wife was unhappy that he spent too much time, and made too little money, in the ashram. Vineet was also a student of computer science. His wife believed that he could have a better future and that he was responsible for the better future of his family too. No salary raise, no offer for extra help, no promise that his swamini made to him could calm down the wife. She wanted him to look for another job.

During my first summer in Takoli, Vineet used to drive me around the area, and he did this with pleasure. He liked showing me his favorite places, and he liked telling me about the young people in the Himalayas. Frequently we had to argue. Vineet belonged to an anti-Gandhi movement that supports some ideas of communism they have, in my view, misunderstood. I had risked my life to flee from communism, and I had published a book describing the grim experience I had living under a totalitarian regime. When this was the topic of our conversations Vineet ironically used to call me *professor*. I did not succeed in convincing Vineet that he did not know enough about communism, but on the whole, he did like me, and he called me *mataji*, mother, more often than *professor*.

One day Vineet took me to a place he had loved since he was a child. It was at the bank of the river Beas. We had to walk down from the road to the water. Just before we stopped, I noticed a small shelter on the right. A holy man, covered only with a loincloth, was standing right in front of it. Around him, sitting cross legged on the ground, there were another seven, eight young men. The holy man was leaning on a broken cane, and he was talking to the young men—quietly but with some passion. The young men were looking up to him and listening.

"This is a wise man," Vineet explained, "and the young men are my friends. We come here often. We built his shelter. We bring him food and blankets, and he teaches us—his wisdom."

The holy man welcomed me in good English, but the young men looked at me with surprise. I let Vineet join the group, and I sat by the water.

The river was quite swift there. I could not follow with my eyes any single point I looked at. It was only possible to see the whole—a portion of the swiftly moving, ever-changing stream.

"That's life too ..." said Vineet behind my back an hour later.

"Will we come again?" I asked.

"Of course," he said. "I am so glad you like this place. Swamini ji has not seen it yet."

We climbed the little hill up to the road in silence.

"Could you actually leave ..." I started to ask.

"Even if I had to leave the job," Vineet replied, "I would never leave Swamini ji. She is such an important part of my life. I will always be there for her."

Vineet and I were planning to write about Swamini ji together. I found the story of their work fascinating but I had not witnessed it, and Vineet had a talent telling me about these epic days. I suggested that he write a book, which I could edit. He promised me to try. In the following year a baby was born into his family. Vineet announced that he was looking for a job. Swamini ji begged him to stay till the end of the winter. She simply could not survive alone, without his help. He promised. One day, he did not come to work. He left for good. He simply did not come again. Swamini ji did not hear from him for a very long time. A year later though, after Swamini ji had accepted the fact that Vineet needed to learn more and to develop professionally, the beautiful relationship between the aging woman and the young man was restored. Swamini ji trusted Vineet completely, and he remained her confidant and esteemed advisor. To him, she was part of his life and his spiritual development, and he was religiously dedicated to helping her as much as he could.

It looked as if the ashram would have to be closed. There was no way for Swamini ji to run it alone.

"The God Mother will help with whatever is the right thing to do," she kept saying in her e-mails to me.

Swamini ji survived the winter. And one day in the spring she said the God Mother sent her a man who was even better than Vineet.

Only a few days after we had arrived at the ashram in Takoli, Esha received a phone call from her uncle. He had received a letter that her visa application was resolved and her passport was supposed to be picked up in Dehradun, the biggest city near Rishikesh.

It was not clear from the letter whether Esha had or had not received the visa. Someone had to go pick up the passport and see what the outcome was. We were very far from Dehradun, about a fourteen-hour drive. It was decided that Nandlal, Esha's father, would go. He was a man, and thus, he could take a bus—something Esha would not have been allowed to do, because such trips were apparently dangerous for women. Nandlal could also stay with one of his brothers in Dehradun, pick up the passport, and take the overnight bus back to Takoli—all could be done in less than two days. Most of all, Nandlal was always ready to do things—anything that was necessary or good for the family. So he did. We sent him off with many instructions and a letter that authorized him to pick up Esha's passport. In about thirty-six hours or so, he came back with his daughter's passport and the letter from the British Consulate. The visa was denied, on the basis of the fact that Esha had no permanent job. The British authorities did not believe her that she honestly wanted to travel to the UK simply for a visit—that was the literal formulation of the explanation. On the back of Esha's passport, there was a stamp showing that a visa to the United Kingdom had been rejected.

"This is like a brand mark," Siddhartha muttered into the silence. What he meant was that in the future, the authorities of any country that Esha might want to visit would always know that she had been denied entry by one of the Western governments.

I had lived for thirty-three years under a totalitarian regime. I felt brand-marked by the lack of the freedom to learn, to write, or even to read what I wanted. I could not legally leave the communist country I was born in and so had to leave illegally, through several borders. Now, in Takoli, I was looking at my young Indian friend being brand-marked by the lack of the freedom to enter the free world for which more than more than quarter of a century ago I had risked my life.

I did not rush into blaming the British authorities, or complaining about their complete misunderstanding of Esha's intentions. I knew all too well that they could have had serious concerns and that any government had the right to determine who may and who may not enter its country. What I was wondering about was what the parameters of freedom really were. Freedom perhaps is a concept we use all too often, without acknowledging that we are actually talking about too many different things, for there is freedom of speech, and freedom of choice, freedom of practicing one's religion, or of wearing a burka, and there are also legal freedoms or liberties, and freedom of mind and of spirit. Apparently, some of those different kinds of freedom have little or nothing to do with each other.

The following summer Amita's son was getting married in Hungary. The whole family was preparing to go to the wedding. I was there with them again, but they did not want to go to Takoli, because they were waiting for their visas and they were shopping for wedding presents. The son had lived in Hungary for many years. He had a completely legal status and a well-paid job as a manager of a big Ayurveda clinic in Budapest. Then I had to leave India unexpectedly, because my mother fell ill. By the time I left, there was still no news about the visas. Later in the summer I learned that the family was not allowed to enter Europe. There was a wedding in Hungary, but at the wedding there was no family.

At the bank of Mother Ganga, at around six-thirty in the morning, Amita cleaned the little altar, lit her candles, and put oil in the oil lamps and on the heads of each of the statues of the gods—Shiva, Ganesha, and Parvati. She pulled her skirts a little and walked barefoot into the river. She bent down, took some holy water in her palms, and washed her face. Then she prayed for her son, who was far away, to be well and happy.

Chapter VIII

The Silent Teacher

In 2014 I hesitated to travel to India. The reasons were primarily financial, but including a trip to India my plans for that particular summer would have also meant to be away from home for a very, very long time. My visit to India had to fit in between my older son's wedding in the Philippines and my stay in London with my husband's family. To save money on tickets, I wanted to have only one return flight to Asia. This, however, would have meant to spend at least two months in India, until the time came to go London. I realize that people spend years in India, but for me two months, at that particular point of my life, was a very long time.

"It is crazy to hang around for two months in India," my son told me, "especially considering the fact that this year you are not going to trek in the Himalayas or to travel around the country, because you do not have the money for all that.

What are you going to do in Rishikesh or in Takoli for two whole months?"

I argued that this particular year I really needed to go to India for two reasons. In the first place, the person I called my teacher, whom I had found only the year before, was not in perfect health. The time I had spent with him a year before was so powerful that I did not want to miss the opportunity to spend another summer with him. Nor did I want him to be disappointed and think that, like many Western tourists, I had a good time in his ashram and then I went back home and forgot all about the tasks he gave me and the promises I made, for I took those tasks and those promises very seriously, and I wanted him to know that.

"I have the chance to be with a very special teacher," I insisted, trying to justify a long trip and a long absence from home.

"If it is not this teacher you will find another one," said my other son. "There are many teachers in the world."

Are there many teachers in the world? thought I to myself. *What is a teacher? What is a master? A guru?*

In my world built upon the fundamental value of diversity of any kind—religious, cultural, ethnic, or racial—and of mutual respect, I should admit that there are many teachers in the world, as there are many paths to spiritual development and many methods to achieving the same spiritual goals. Nevertheless, I had to disagree with what some of the people close to me were telling me—that I could always find another teacher. Such statements made me contemplate on the question of why I believed that this one particular man I had met only a year ago was the only living teacher I could have.

I am not a fanatic. Just the opposite—fanaticism has always scared me to death, and I have run away from anything in my life that looked remotely like fanaticism. Nor have I ever been overexcited by people, teachings, places, or relationships. By nature, I am a philosopher, an analyst. I tend to look carefully at everything that comes my way and to make my choices slowly. Excitement is not my mode of existence.

I was fortunate to have the profound spiritual teachings of a real master as the solid basis of my entire life, of the Master Beinsa Douno. This meant that I was content with my views and my life, that I was not in search for another kind of guidance, and that I was definitely not jumping from the fascination with one esoteric school of thought to the fascination with another. However, all this did not mean that I had stopped learning. My character, my upbringing, and the teachings of my master formed me as a person who worships studying, learning, and teaching—most particularly of human thought and of our perception of spirituality. I never stopped learning about different philosophical and religious traditions, nor have I stopped looking for ways to develop on deeper spiritual levels. But the thought that I never had a living teacher had not even come to my mind in the past. I never thought of the master I had in terms of a living or a non-living master. His presence in my life was simply a reality. Once in a while, when I was very young, and I was trekking in the mountains through the places where the Master used to camp with his disciples in the summer, I felt sad that I had not been there to share those precious moments.

In my days, the followers of Beinsa Douno were strictly forbidden by the communist regime to camp or to get together anywhere in the Bulgarian mountains. So, I had no experience of listening to the living words of this teacher, of spending time in a retreat with him, or of being guided in my practices. Later in my life, I learned that a direct disciple could play the role of a living teacher, and I was glad that I had that experience. I was taught by a direct disciple indeed. Instead of having what people today call retreats, I was spending many hours every week, almost every day, with this wonderful person whose love for his master allowed him to achieve the highest possible degree of immediacy in conveying

Beinsa Douno's teachings, views, practical advice, and deep, esoteric understanding of many spiritual questions. Did I then have a teacher?

I asked myself this question only recently. Eventually, at the age of fifty-nine, after having been on what people call a spiritual path for about forty-six years, I had found my living teacher—unexpectedly, as a complete surprise, without searching for one. When I found him in one of the most beautiful places I have known, in the Center for the Study of the Himalayan yoga tradition, the Swami Rama Sadhaka Grama Meditation Center in Rishikesh, this exceptional man had just given a vow of five years of silence.

"How does he teach you?" asked my husband when I told him briefly about that.

This was the question that made me ask myself what a teacher really was. My husband's question, I believe, is at the core of the understanding of the phenomenon of a spiritual teacher or a guru, as they say in India. If there is anything taught and anything learned, then there is a teacher and there is a disciple. The greatness of the teacher does not depend, I think, on anything else but the greatness of the thing taught. When or where the teacher lives may not matter much. How s/he lives matters because it is relevant to the thing taught. The question that is left then is how the thing is taught.

The word, both spoken and written, is a powerful mediator. From my first master I learned mostly by reading the shorthand records of lectures he had given at the time and by listening to one of his disciples. Was that only an intellectual path of learning? I would say no—it was not. In the environment I learned about these teachings, with the constant house raids for his incriminated books, having to hide when we were more than two like-minded people gathering in one place, being afraid to share my views with anyone, including with the members of my own family, I believe that there was a lot of spiritual practice involved, in addition to the intellectual comprehension of the texts. I was constantly put to the test, and I had to practice what I studied in order to preserve not only my convictions but my normal daily life. And now, my teacher in India was silent.

He, of course, had written many scholarly books on the *Yoga Sutras*, on meditation, and on many other spiritual topics. In the first year of his silence, he also gave a whole course, using computer technology. I had not attended that course, but I read several of his books. Was I supposed to tell my husband that my teacher who keeps his silence vow was teaching through a computer? Or that he was teaching me through his books—a method I was quite well acquainted with. I knew that something would be wrong with such an answer. It simply would not be true. It took me some time to realize what my answer should have been.

A year earlier, after I had shared with Swami Veda the brief history of my spiritual development, he made an incredible gesture, a gesture on a grand scale that only a real master could make. Among many other things, I mentioned to him that I had not had a living master and that I had not been initiated. It had never crossed my mind that I could be initiated, nor that Swami Veda could become my teacher. In some way, however, a master, when s/he is a real master, knows what a seeker thinks or feels, what s/he lacks, desires, or dreams of. I have always been content with not having been initiated in any particular tradition. To me, this was something for another life. That thought, however, did make me sad. Deep down, I was always dreaming of that mystical experience of being in the presence of a master—here and now. Most of all, I had been dreaming of sharing, through initiation, that universal, all-embracing love that bring us all together, the love that some call God. Swami Veda, being a master, knew that. He must have felt how much I needed such experience and how much it would have meant to me. And he decided to make a sacrifice. He broke his silence once—to initiate me. He did this for me, a nobody—someone who came to him from nowhere, someone who was going to leave and who might never have come again. Or perhaps he made a sacrifice for a human being who was in real need?

How do I explain what Swami Veda's sacrifice taught me? Have I been ready to sacrifice that much for anyone except maybe for my children? What have I been ready to sacrifice? How was I making sacrifices? Why? For whom? Did I expect anything in return when I made a sacrifice? Did I have any second thoughts? What were my reasons to compromise with anything? Would I have done anything like that for someone who may even forget what I had done for them? There are so many more questions I have been asking myself, that arose in my mind because of the extraordinary act of Swami Veda.

In the year following my initiation, I came back to Rishikesh. I wanted to spend most of the time around Swami ji in the Sadhaka Grama, the village for seekers. In the first place, I needed to be in the presence of my teacher. To be in the presence of a master is a mystical experience that I am not able to explain, but I knew I badly needed that experience again. Around Swami ji I felt as if I was in a space of the pure good. It was as if I had another version of me, a modified version, an extension or a squared me—with bigger lungs and cleaner and clearer thoughts, healthier, calmer, more peaceful, more loving, and certainly more forgiving. I also knew that Swami ji had expected me to return. I did not want him to think even for a moment that I would disappoint him. How often do we all say to our friends that we will call them and we do not? That we will be in touch and we are not? That we will see them soon, and then we let years pass before we remember when we saw them last?

Did I learn to keep my word? Or did I learn to care? Or to feel the obligation of someone who was on the receiving end?

I have a niece who works as a mountain guide. She told me once that all the people in her groups who have had trouble during treks and needed help ended up hating her and complaining about her at the end.

"They could not look me in the eye," she said. "People often hate those who help them because they hate being seen when they are weak. Their big fat ego stands in the way of simple gratitude."

Did I learn from my teacher to feel genuinely grateful for the help, for the spiritual support? I think I did, but I don't know how exactly. Swami ji never requested anything. A master has the authority to require just about anything on the spiritual level—action, behavior, attention. But Swami ji was silent, and I was thousands of miles away—at the other end of the world. There were several e-mail exchanges between us during the year. I was far from India when I learned endless lessons through each one of them. When I returned eventually, in the summer of 2014, I started to realize what the teaching process between me and Swami ji was.

Swami ji learned that I was able to afford staying in the ashram only for a few days. He learned it directly from me, as well as from another person who was part of his spiritual family, someone who wanted to help me and who probably always wants to help—the publisher of the monthly journal *Ahymsin*. Surely, Swami ji knew I needed to be around him, and despite the fact that he was ill and he was in silence, he found the time and the strength to make arrangements for me. I was invited to stay in the Sadhaka Grama as long as I wished and pay as much as I could. Many of my big dreams were fulfilled in this life—not without my effort, and yet—how many people can say that they have lived their dreams? Studying and practicing in the meditation center and being around Swami ji was one of my dreams. I was feeling blessed.

Before I moved to the village of seekers, I was staying with my friend Siddhartha, as usual. Swami ji had written to me that he was going deeper and deeper into silence but that he was still sitting on the evening meditation for about an hour. This, in his words, was his only contact with the outside world at the moment. So, every evening, I was taking a rickshaw to go the Sadhaka Grama for the meditation.

We gathered always in the main hall—twenty, maybe thirty people—not sure. I was so happy that I could sit there, in the presence of Swami Veda. I could actually share this hour of meditation with him and all these amazing people who lived in the ashram and to whom being together in meditation was a necessary part of life. I knew this was the closest contact I was going to have with Swami ji—this summer and maybe ever.

One evening I arrived in the center too early. I was sitting on a bench in front of the meditation hall, waiting for people to start gathering. A small group appeared, walking slowly toward me from the other corner of the building. One of them was pushing a wheelchair. It was Swami ji being brought to the meditation hall. I jumped on my feet and backed up so I was not in the way. Swami ji looked straight at me, tilted his head toward his left shoulder, as he often used to do, and smiled. His face was shining, as if illuminated. His smile was wide, happy, and gentle. I put my hands together in front of my chest, as if for a prayer, and I closed my eyes for a second.

Thank you, thank you for everything, for letting me come, for being here with me, for seeing you, for everything ... I thought.

I opened my eyes. There was more I wanted to

express, a lot more. I now spontaneously crossed my arms in front of my heart as if I was embracing all my feelings for my teacher, all my admiration, all my respect, all gratitude, in fact all my deep love that filled my heart.

Thank you for this experience of love, I thought.

Swami ji lifted his right hand from his lap and put it over his heart—still illuminated in a smile. For a brief moment, we were face-to-face with each other, both smiling, and both embracing each other in our hearts. I was illuminated too, I thought. What was the light that covered me? Swami ji's love for his disciples, for me, for all human beings? Not only. It was not only the love for anything or anyone. It was that love that is a state of being. And for a brief moment in my life, Swami ji had taken me along to that state. I had felt, experienced, and realized it, and there was no power in the world that could have ever taken it from me. I may not be able to get back to that state on my own, but I can dream of it and aim at it. I knew then that even on the days when darkness may envelop my thoughts, when fear and despair may prevail, I could close my eyes and move up into the light of Swami ji's embrace of love.

It never crossed my mind to utter a word. Can words express what happened in that moment? I cannot find those words perhaps, but I know that what happened that evening was going to stay with me in this and in many other worlds.

The presence of a real master is a mystical experience. The presence of a silent master, who can teach you in his silence, is a blessing and an unending source of life and love. If we could only learn!

Chapter IX

Before I managed to arrange my stay in the Sadhaka Grama, Swami ji was taken to a hospital in Delhi. In the ashram, they said that he was going just for some tests and that he would be back soon, but I realized that no one really knew when exactly he was coming back.

I decided to remain in my usual lodging, the Ganga Sadan, where I was always welcome with Siddhartha and his mother. I was used to that place. I knew the people who worked there, I relied on good non-spicy food, prepared by two beautiful and warmhearted women. I had settled in a room that was a bit hot, because it was just under the roof, but that had a terrace overlooking the Ganga. Given the fact that my teacher was not going to be there, it seemed unnecessary to move to the Sadhaka Grama.

Gradually, as the first couple of weeks passed,

I began to realize that something had changed in Rishikesh, but I could not put my finger on it.

Siddhartha had moved from the little house next to the ashram to an unfinished building up the hill, in the middle of the jungle. His father, Prabhuji, could no longer stand the noise in the city and wanted to live in peace and quiet, out in the open, to feel nature all around. Rishikesh had become unbearably busy, noisy, and polluted. I had known this place as a beautiful small town at the Mother Ganga, that got busy only once a year, when pilgrims started walking toward the source of the holy river, up the mountains in the Garhwal region. I knew that the town was also busy during the bathing gathering of the Half Kumbh Mela that happened only once every few years. Now, the city had changed into a relatively cheap destination for Delhi weekenders. Both foreigners and Indians were organizing rafting holidays, boy-scout camps, beach outings, and all sorts of other events that bring the city a lot of business and a lot of dirt. Trekking and rafting agencies, cafés, restaurants offering Western-style cuisine, fresh juice stands, yoga, meditation, and massage schools, shops for Ayurveda medications and cosmetics, and stores for gems from all around the world were popping up on the narrow streets by the hour. Only three years earlier, the back road that led along the river between the Ram Jhula and the Laxman Jhula hanging bridges used to be a quiet dirt road with a few shops and cafés, but populated mostly by poor people, holy men who had no shelter, street dogs, meager cows, and macaque monkeys. One might have been able to see other tourists there once in a while, but there were certainly no crowds. This year the same road was much cleaner, and it was full of Internet cafés, German bakeries, and Indian and Tibetan shops selling high-quality knit work and sports goods. The crowd was immense. Obviously the shopkeepers were making money. There must have been jobs available to more people than before. Did I see that as progress? I have to admit that I did. I saw it as rapid economic progress. However, the speed with which the economy of this city was growing was out of proportion with the change of mentality. Hygiene, sustainability, or pollution were all concepts that were not yet discussed by the appropriate administrative institutions and that very few people cared about in their daily lives. There was an international initiative to promote keeping the holy river clean that began with an appeal by Parmarth Niketan, the largest ashram in Rishikesh, but no change was visible yet.

My friend Siddhartha was quite upset about the fast economic growth of the city and most particularly about the rapid development of tourism. One Sunday he took his father to a beach they used to go to when Siddhartha was a little boy. This was the place of the confluence of the rivers Ganga and Gular. In Hindu tradition a place where two rivers meet is sacred. People go to such places as a pilgrimage. They pray, meditate in silence, and enjoy the divinity of nature. That Sunday, Siddhartha came back from the outing sad and angry.

"The beach," he said, "was not only overcrowded and dirty, but it had turned into an area where teenage boys bring their girlfriends on weekends in order to have premarital sex secretly. I do not mind seeing lovers—there are so many beautiful descriptions of love-couples in our mythology. But I do mind the condom and the hashish sellers walking around, and the way a sacred space is turned into a marketplace for cheap and vulgar attitudes."

This was appalling to him. In his eyes it meant not only desecrating the place but also destroying tradition. He shared his disappointment on his Facebook. Some people disagreed. Their argument was that tourism and economy ought to develop, and that we needed to move with the times.

Was that a necessary contradiction, I wondered.

The question was difficult. It made me think about London, my second home. Tourism in this metropolis has flooded certain parts of the city, such as Leicester Square or Oxford Street, with too many visitors, so that I cannot bear walking there, particularly not in summertime. The café that was opened in the crypt of St. Paul's, with its tables standing on top of centuries-old graves, so that one could read the names of those buried there while sipping café latte, was also a bit much for me and for many others. Nevertheless, teenagers were not having sex on the steps of St. Paul's, and there were no condom sellers in the garden of Westminster Abbey. At least I have never seen this.

Some compromises with customs and tradition, for the sake of any kind of progress, may be inevitable. We may need to accept the changes in the way people dress or in the way they greet each other. We probably are forced to adjust to the new way we converse, being constantly interrupted by phone calls or text messages on our mobile phones. In some of these cases we feel that we compromise with our traditional views and in others we adapt to the new ways so quickly that we do not even realize they contradict what we used to believe in. But there must be some limits in accepting compromises for the sake of adjusting to a new world. Otherwise we will begin to destroy the world that was already built. If humanity had destroyed one by one all old beliefs, traditional values, customs, or ideas of virtues, then we would not have even known that they had existed. We have to preserve something in order to have culture, religion, and history. Adopting the new has to go hand in hand with preserving the old—even if only to a degree. This is a basic fact in the development of science, of philosophy, of politics, and of much more. It is logical that it would be a natural process in society too.

In India, traditionally mountain peaks, caves, or rivers are seen as sacred, even as gods. Economic and technological progress does not always have to happen at the expense of respect for tradition. But to have progress and tradition go hand in hand, there has to be a lot of effort put into educating society. And society consists of everyone. So education has to reach everybody. This is a question of the societal relations between people. Whose responsibility is educating society? I believe that those who have the information, the knowledge, the know-how, or the skills are the ones who should have the responsibility to actively reach out to those who don't—rather than the other way round.

That summer I thought that if anything destroys old India and its spiritual beauty, it will not be the economic and the technological progress of the country. Rather, it might be the clash between culture and religious or spiritual beliefs. As with so many other cases, it seems that culture wins. In an *honor-shame* based society, paying attention to public opinion more than to the issues at stake inevitably leads to an anomaly—it leads to pretense. Whether one follows tradition, rituals, religious principles, or customs to "please" others or whether one disregards them for the same reason does not make any difference. The result is the same—we begin to pretend. I realized that the question of *honor-shame* behavior has very deep roots in Hindu mythology too. In the Bhagavad-Gita Krishna tells Arjuna: "And your enemies will speak many indecent words while denigrating your might. What can be more painful than that?"[3] This statement, however, is believed to contradict the real message of the epics. Elsewhere in the text, adherence to local customs, family, or traditions is considered an impure feeling because it expresses the fear of being censured by others and the Gita is fundamentally against "pleasing the world" and considers such behavior "not conducive to the human goal."[4] Nevertheless, for some reason the need for people to please others, in order to see themselves esteemed by public opinion, seems to trump some of the most profound religious and spiritual principles. I saw ashrams where some people are not allowed to enter because they are not real ashramites, because

---

[3] Madhusudana Sarasvati. *Bhagavad-Gita*. Calcutta, 2000, sloka 2.36, 160.
[4] Ibid., 452–3.

they do not meditate, or because they practice an "improper" type of yoga. There is powerful fear that one could damage the reputation of the ashram, of the family, or of the community or one's own reputation. I was wondering if such fear does not go against the fundamental idea of the unity of Brahman, the essence of the universe, and Atman, the essence of the individual self, an idea accepted by most Hindu schools of thought.[5] The same question applies when a temple does not allow a Hindu to enter because he has a white wife or when a man, who badly needs a job to support his family, refuses to clean toilets because he comes from a family of Brahmins. That man would not lose face in front of the villagers, but he would let his family go hungry. My friend Siddhartha never mentions the fact that he comes from a Brahmin family. He does not want to involve his heritage in his life or in his teachings. In my view, to have a Brahmin heritage should matter as little as to be a Chandala. Despite the fact that the scriptures say Brahman, the supreme Self, and Atman, the individual self, are the same, I could see a Chandala on every step in India and I could see people pretend to follow principles that they

---

[5] Consider for example Shankaracharya's tale of Chandala, or the Mandukya Upanishad

dropped every time when their reputation was at stake.

In the West, where plenty of people are treated as Chandala too, there is a view of India as a whole that is very different from the one I present in this book. Many of my friends wonder why I go to India every year. They tell me that I idealize a country that, seen from a societal perspective, is quite imperfect. They criticize the inability of Indian society to deal with the inherent view of castes, despite the legally enforced process of reservation. They do not see enough progress with regard to the way women, the largest part of the population, are being treated. They are horrified by the level of poverty the country has to deal with. I know so well how right they are. I know well for how long India has been struggling to reform. Despite all that, however, I also see that on some of India's many, many levels of existence, there is hidden spiritual depth, wisdom, purity, and innocence, and there is love. I am not a Hindu scholar, and I cannot say if many of the problems of contemporary Indian society are a consequence of the beliefs at the foundation of Hinduism itself. Nor do I pretend to know the roots of the issues Indian society has today. I certainly do not know everything that is going on behind the scene in the schools and the ashrams I have been visiting either. But my conviction is that the capacity of the human mind allows us to choose living a mindful life. The individual human intellect and the spirit each one of us bears are in charge of making choices. From the vast pool of ideas and beliefs that every culture, every religion, and every scripture has, we could select only those ideas and beliefs that touch us personally and that make us feel that we are on a path to something good, positive, compassionate, and constructive. I am deeply convinced that every path is right when it leads to the good, and that in every single religion there are elements that could be misread, misinterpreted, or misused for the purpose of something destructive. The spiritual culture in the Indian Himalaya, as I see it, is a treasure trove of diverse methods for the development of mindful living. With my eyes fully open, I chose to focus on the rare beauty I found in that culture. Its beauty may be as rare as the blue poppies in the high hills of the Himalaya but I see it as a source of good, a source of compassion, a source of understanding ourselves and humanity. We ought to keep some of these sources pristine, like pure water. Someday we might need to tap into them as if into a precious artesian spring, when the rest of the earth shows no more signs of fresh water supplies.

I always wanted to share my India with my younger son. Both my sons have been very close to me, but my younger son understood better my dedication to spiritual development. In addition, he and I have always been great travel companions. He is also a mountaineer with a lot more experience than me, and I wanted to trek with him in the Himalaya. But ever since I had started going to India, this had been a plan impossible to realize. Both my sons were working very hard, switching jobs and living in different places, and they could never take a vacation that was long enough in order to spend time with me in India. In 2013, however, my younger son and I were both going to visit his brother, who was living in Hong Kong at the time. We met in Delhi and spent a few days there before we flew to Hong Kong. There was no time to show my son the mountains or Rishikesh, but at least he could get a glimpse of Delhi and the Taj Mahal.

I booked a day tour to Agra and the Taj by bus, remembering how interesting my first bus trip had been many years ago. Back then, however, I went to Agra during the high season, and I had a fancy tourist bus, full of people from all around the world. We went straight to Agra, stopping only for lunch in a nice luxury hotel. This time, when my son came, the season was over. It was already too hot. When we got on the bus, we realized that we would be traveling with Indian pilgrims and that we would be going not only to the Taj Mahal but also to two other religious sites. We had to take back roads, and the trip lasted forever. The restaurant where we stopped for lunch served very spicy Indian food—there were no choices available. I ate only rice, and my son got a bad tummy from the food. That evening, when we were back in our hotel, I asked carefully how he liked the trip—being afraid that it was all too much for him.

"It was fabulous," he said. "Thank God we traveled with locals and not with foreign tourists and that we went to see those other temples that were important to them. This gave me the feeling that I saw something more authentic—not just tourist sites. I want to think that I have seen a bit of the real India."

I was so happy that my son tried to understand a little ... though we, people from the West, can never really understand India. But I loved India and I loved my son, and it was so good that the two of them had come together. Would he ever come again for long—to study, to live with its people the way I did, to trek in the Himalaya, or to meditate at the banks of the Ganga? Would I ever return as planned?

On the way back from Agra, the bus took the new express road. I did not know it had been built. Years ago, when I first went to see the Taj, we took the old Agra road, where we saw slums of animals and people, road circuses with disabled children being shown for pocket money, snake charmers, and trees heavy with monkeys. I had hoped my son would see the same—it was part of real India. But the expressway was running in the middle of a vast empty land. There was nothing to see on either side—for hours. One could only see the sky and the sunset before it got dark. My son was napping in his seat. In my mind the images of the India I knew were taking turns in convincing me how much I loved being there. I saw the tea leaf pickers in Darjeeling, with their colorful umbrellas; the Himalayan blue poppies across the Indus River ridge; I saw Amita stepping into the waters of Mother Ganga to pray; I heard Siddhartha sing in the temple in Takoli; I saw my silent teacher smile at me among the roses in the village of seekers; and I felt the icy air sneaking into my sleeping bag in the tent at the Shangri la pass. The road was taking me back to Delhi, and I was going to fly to Hong Kong on the next morning. But India was in my blood. It has grown on me as moss grows on a rock, and it has changed me. Loving it seemed to have made it my world and I realized that I could never really leave it. What I have learned in India has given me more than any other experience in my life. The people who taught me will be with me every hour, every day—no matter where I am. The country, as I know it, is a space in my mind to which I always will be returning. My teacher, Swami Veda, taught me to believe in the endless power of the mind. Through a focused, one-pointed mind, it is possible to reach *Samadhi*, the state of union between the inner-self and God. If that is possible, then I should always be able to reach India in me.